Machine Learning for Streaming Data with Python

Rapidly build practical online machine learning
solutions using River and other top key frameworks

Joos Korstanje

BIRMINGHAM—MUMBAI

Machine Learning for Streaming Data with Python

Publishing Product Manager: Dinesh Chaudhary
Content Development Editor: Joseph Sunil
Technical Editor: Rahul Limbachiya
Copy Editor: Safis Editing
Project Coordinator: Farheen Fathima
Proofreader: Safis Editing
Indexer: Sejal Dsilva
Production Designer: Shankar Kalbhor
Marketing Coordinator: Shifa Ansari and Abeer Riyaz Dawe

First published: July 2022

Production reference: 1240622

Published by Packt Publishing Ltd.
Livery Place
35 Livery Street
Birmingham
B3 2PB, UK.

ISBN 978-1-80324-836-3

www.packt.com

Contributors

About the author

Joos Korstanje, with his master's degrees in both environmental sciences and data science, has been working on statistics and data science for almost 10 years. Through his work in different companies including Disney, AXA, and others, he has closely followed developments in data science and related fields. This experience in the business world has allowed him to write about data science from an applied point of view (through his books, Medium, Towards Data Science, LinkedIn, and more).

About the reviewer

Olivia Petris is a big data engineer working as an IT consultant in a technology and advisory services firm based in Paris. On her professional journey, she's always looking for challenging and interesting assignments. Since her engineering diploma in computer science, she has chosen to be in the data science and big data field. Therefore, she continues to improve her skills and keep up to date with new IT and technology developments. In her free time, she enjoys traveling, practicing karate, and hanging out with her family and friends.

Table of Contents

3

Data Analysis on Streaming Data

Part 2: Exploring Use Cases for Data Streaming

4

Online Learning with River

5

Online Anomaly Detection

6

Online Classification

7

Online Regression

8

Reinforcement Learning

Part 3: Advanced Concepts and Best Practices around Streaming Data

9

Drift and Drift Detection

10

Feature Transformation and Scaling

11

Catastrophic Forgetting

12

Conclusion and Best Practices

Other Books You May Enjoy

Preface

Streaming data is the new top technology to watch in the field of data science and machine learning. As business needs become more demanding, many use cases require real-time analysis as well as real-time machine learning. This book will allow you to get up to speed with data analytics for streaming data and focuses strongly on adapting machine learning and other analytics to the case of streaming data.

You will first learn about the architecture for streaming and real-time machine learning. You will then look at the state-of-the-art frameworks for streaming data such as River.

You will learn about various industrial use cases for streaming data, such as online anomaly detection. Then, you will deep dive into challenges and how you will mitigate them. You will then learn the best practices that will help you use streaming data to generate real-time insights.

Upon completion of the book, you will be confident about using streaming data in your machine learning models.

Who this book is for

Data scientists and machine learning engineers who have a basis in machine learning, are practice- and technology-oriented, and want to learn how to apply machine learning to streaming data through practical examples with modern technologies will benefit from this book. You will need to understand basic Python and machine learning concepts but require no prior knowledge of streaming.

What this book covers

Chapter 1, Introduction to Streaming Data, explains what streaming data is and why it is different from batch data. This chapter also explains the challenges that we should expect to encounter as well as the advantages of using streaming data.

Chapter 2, Architectures for Streaming and Real-Time Machine Learning, describes various architectures that can be used to set up streaming, and how they can be utilized.

Chapter 3, Data Analysis on Streaming Data, explores data analysis on streaming data, which includes real-time insights, real-time descriptive statistics, real-time visualizations, and basic alerting systems.

Chapter 4, Online Learning with River, covers the core concepts of online learning and also introduces you to the River library, which is a fundamental part of streaming.

Chapter 5, Online Anomaly Detection, covers online anomaly detection, explains how it is useful, and also provides a use case that involves building a program for detecting anomalies in streaming data.

Chapter 6, Online Classification, covers online classification, explains how it is useful, and also provides a use case that involves building a program for classifying streaming data.

Chapter 7, Online Regression, covers online regression, how it is useful, and also provides a use case that involves building a program for detecting regression in streaming data.

Chapter 8, Reinforcement Learning, introduces you to reinforcement learning. We will explore some of the key algorithms and also explore some use cases for it using Python.

Chapter 9, Drift and Drift Detection, focuses on helping us understand drift in online learning and learning how to build solutions to detect drift.

Chapter 10, Feature Transformation and Scaling, shows us how to build a feature transformation pipeline that works with real-time and streaming data.

Chapter 11, Catastrophic Forgetting, explores what catastrophic forgetting is, and shows us how we can deal with it using example use cases.

Chapter 12, Conclusion and Best Practices, acts as a review of the book and combines all the concepts explored throughout the book for us to revise and revisit as needed.

To get the most out of this book

For following along with this book, you can use online notebook environments like Google Colab, Kaggle Notebooks, or your own local Jupyter Notebook environment with Python 3. Also, a (free) AWS account would be needed for a small number of exercises.

Software/hardware covered in the book	Operating system requirements
Python 3	Windows/Linux/Mac
AWS Cloud	Windows/Linux/Mac

If you are using the digital version of this book, we advise you to type the code yourself or access the code from the book's GitHub repository (a link is available in the next section). Doing so will help you avoid any potential errors related to the copying and pasting of code.

Download the example code files

You can download the example code files for this book from GitHub at `https://github.com/PacktPublishing/Machine-Learning-for-Streaming-Data-with-Python`. If there's an update to the code, it will be updated in the GitHub repository.

We also have other code bundles from our rich catalog of books and videos available at `https://github.com/PacktPublishing/`. Check them out!

Download the color images

We also provide a PDF file that has color images of the screenshots and diagrams used in this book. You can download it here: `https://packt.link/6rZ0m`.

Conventions used

There are a number of text conventions used throughout this book.

`Code in text`: Indicates code words in text, database table names, folder names, filenames, file extensions, pathnames, dummy URLs, user input, and Twitter handles. Here is an example: "There is no predict_many function here, so it is necessary to do a loop with predict_one repeatedly."

A block of code is set as follows:

```
def self_made_decision_tree(observation):
    if observation.can_speak:
        if not observation.has_feathers:
            return 'human'
    return 'not human'
for i,row in data.iterrows():
    print(self_made_decision_tree(row))
```

When we wish to draw your attention to a particular part of a code block, the relevant lines or items are set in bold:

```
from sklearn.datasets import make _ blobs
X,y=make _ blobs(shuffle=True,centers=2,n _ samples=2000)
```

Bold: Indicates a new term, an important word, or words that you see onscreen. For instance, words in menus or dialog boxes appear in **bold**. Here is an example: "Select **System info** from the **Administration** panel."

> Tips or important notes
> Appear like this.

Get in touch

Feedback from our readers is always welcome.

General feedback: If you have questions about any aspect of this book, email us at customercare@packtpub.com and mention the book title in the subject of your message.

Errata: Although we have taken every care to ensure the accuracy of our content, mistakes do happen. If you have found a mistake in this book, we would be grateful if you would report this to us. Please visit www.packtpub.com/support/errata and fill in the form.

Piracy: If you come across any illegal copies of our works in any form on the internet, we would be grateful if you would provide us with the location address or website name. Please contact us at copyright@packt.com with a link to the material.

If you are interested in becoming an author: If there is a topic that you have expertise in and you are interested in either writing or contributing to a book, please visit authors.packtpub.com.

Share Your Thoughts

Once you've read *Machine Learning for Streaming Data with Python*, we'd love to hear your thoughts! Scan the QR code below to go straight to the Amazon review page for this book and share your feedback.

https://packt.link/r/1-803-24836-X

Your review is important to us and the tech community and will help us make sure we're delivering excellent quality content.

Part 1: Introduction and Core Concepts of Streaming Data

In this introductory part of the book, we will be introduced to the basic concept and principles surrounding streaming data. We will explore the various architectures that can be used to implement streaming data for machine learning. Finally, we will learn how to do data analysis on streaming data, along with various other functions.

This section comprises the following chapters:

1

An Introduction to Streaming Data

Streaming analytics is one of the new hot topics in data science. It proposes an alternative framework to the more standard batch processing, in which we are no longer dealing with datasets on a fixed time of treatment, but rather we are handling every individual data point directly upon reception.

This new paradigm has important consequences for data engineering, as it requires much more robust and, particularly, much faster data ingestion pipelines. It also imposes a big change in data analytics and machine learning.

Until recently, machine learning and data analytics methods and algorithms were mainly designed to work on entire datasets. Now that streaming has become a hot topic, it becomes more and more common to see use cases in which entire datasets just do not exist anymore. When a continuous stream of data is being ingested into a data storage source, there is no natural moment to relaunch an analytics batch job.

Streaming analytics and streaming machine learning models are models that are designed to work specifically with streaming data sources. A part of the solution, for example, is in the updating. Streaming analytics and machine learning need to update all the time as new data is being received. When updating, you may also want to forget the much older data.

This and other problems that are introduced by moving from batch analytics to streaming analytics need a different approach to analytics and machine learning. This book will lay out the basis for getting you started with data analytics and machine learning on data that is received as a continuous stream.

In this first chapter, you'll get a more solid understanding of the differences between streaming and batch data. You'll see some example use cases that showcase the importance of working with streaming rather than converting back into batch. You'll also start working with a first Python example to get a feel for the type of work that you'll be doing throughout this book.

In later chapters, you'll see some more background notions on architecture and, then, you'll go into a number of data science and analytics use cases and how they can be adapted to the new streaming paradigm.

In this chapter, you will discover the following topics:

- A short history of data science

- Working with streaming data

- Real-time data formats and importing an example dataset in Python

Technical requirements

You can find all the code for this book on GitHub at the following link: `https://github.com/PacktPublishing/Machine-Learning-for-Streaming-Data-with-Python`. If you are not yet familiar with Git and GitHub, the easiest way to download the notebooks and code samples is the following:

1. Go to the link of the repository.

2. Go to the green **Code** button.

3. Select **Download ZIP**:

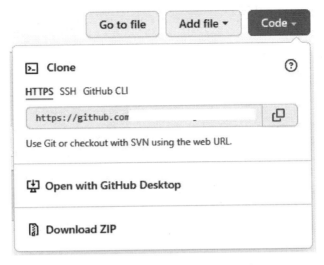

Figure 1.1 – GitHub interface example

When you download the ZIP file, you unzip it in your local environment, and you will be able to access the code through your preferred Python editor.

Setting up a Python environment

To follow along with this book, you can download the code in the repository and execute it using your preferred Python editor.

If you are not yet familiar with Python environments, I would advise you to check out Anaconda (`https://www.anaconda.com/products/individual`), which comes with the Jupyter Notebook and JupyterLab, which are both great for executing notebooks. It also comes with Spyder and VSCode for editing scripts and programs.

If you have difficulty installing Python or the associated programs on your machine, you can check out Google Colab (`https://colab.research.google.com/`) or Kaggle Notebooks (`https://www.kaggle.com/code`), which both allow you to run Python code in online notebooks for free, without any setup to do.

> **Note**
>
> The code in the book will generally use Colab and Kaggle Notebooks with Python version 3.7.13 and you can set up your own environment to mimic this.

A short history of data science

Over the last few years, new technology domains have quickly taken over a lot of parts of the world. Machine learning, artificial intelligence, and data science are new fields that have entered our daily life, both in our personal lives and in our professional lives.

The topics that data scientists work on today are not new. The absolute foundation of the field is in mathematics and statistics, two fields that have existed for centuries. As an example, least squares regression was first published in 1805. With time, mathematicians and statisticians have continued working on finding other methods and models.

In the following timeline, you can see how the recent boom in technology has been able to take place. In the 1600s and 1700s, very smart people were already laying the foundations for what we still do in statistics and mathematics today. However, it was not until the invention and popularization of computing power that the field became booming.

A brief history of data

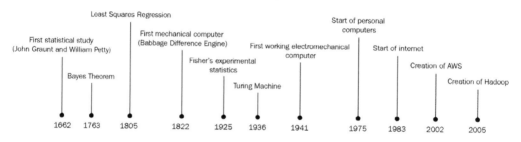

Figure 1.2 – A timeline of the history of data

Personal computer and internet accessibility is an important reason for data science's popularity today. Almost everyone has a computer that is performant enough for fairly complex machine learning. This strongly helps computer literacy, but also, online documentation accessibility is a big booster for learning.

The availability of big data tools such as **Hadoop** and **Spark** is also an important part of the popularization of data science, as they allow practitioners to work with datasets that are larger than anyone could ever imagine before.

Lastly, **cloud computing** is allowing data scientists from all over the world to access very powerful hardware at low prices. Especially for big data tools, the hardware needed is still priced in a way that most students would not be able to buy it for training purposes. Cloud computing gives access to those use cases for many.

In this book, you will learn how to work with **streaming data**. It is important to have this short history of data science in mind, as streaming data is one of those technologies that has been disadvantaged by the need for difficult hardware and setup requirements. Streaming data is currently gaining popularity quickly in many domains and has the potential to be a big hit in the coming period. Let's now have a deeper look into the definition of streaming data.

Working with streaming data

Streaming data is data that is streamed. You may know the term **streaming** from online video services on which you can stream video. When doing this, the video streaming service will continue sending the next parts of the video to you while you are already watching the first part of the video.

The concept is the same when working with streaming data. The data format is not necessarily video and can be any data type that is useful for your use case. One of the most intuitive examples is that of an industrial production line, in which you have continuous measurements from sensors. As long as your production line doesn't pause, you will continue to generate measurements. We will check out the following overview of the data streaming process:

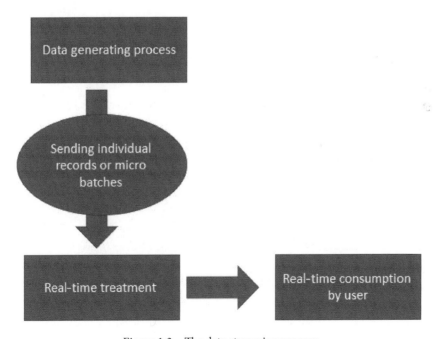

Figure 1.3 – The data streaming process

The important notion is that you have a continuous flow of data that you need to treat in real time. You cannot wait until the production line stops to do your analysis, as you would need to detect potential problems right away.

Streaming data versus batch data

Streaming data is generally not among the first use cases that new data scientists tend to start with. The type of problem that is usually introduced first is batch use cases. Batch data is the opposite of streaming data, as it works in **phases**: you collect a bunch of data, and then you treat a bunch of data.

If you see streaming data as streaming a video online, you could see batch data as downloading the entire video first and then watching it when the downloading is finished. For analytical purposes, this would mean that you get the analysis of a bunch of data when the data generating process is finished rather than whenever a problem occurs.

For some use cases, this is not a problem. Yet, you can understand that streaming can deliver great added value in those use cases where fast analytics can have an impact. It also has added value in use cases where data is ingested in a streaming method, which is becoming more and more common. In practice, many use cases that would get added value through streaming are still solved with batch treatment, just because these methods are better known and more widespread.

The following overview shows the batch treatment process:

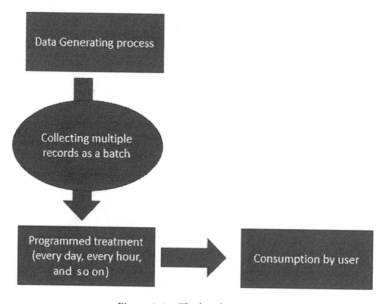

Figure 1.4 – The batch process

Advantages of streaming data

Let's now look at some advantages of using streaming analytics rather than other approaches in the following subsections.

Data generating processes are in real time

The first advantage of building streaming data analytics rather than batch systems is that many data generating processes are actually in real time. You will discover a number of use cases later, but in general, it is rare that data collection is done in batches.

Although most of us are used to building batch systems around real-time data generating systems, it often makes more sense to build streaming analytics directly.

Of course, batch analytics and streaming analytics can co-exist. Yet, adding a batch treatment to a streaming analytics service is often much easier than adding streaming functionality into a system that is designed for batches. It simply makes the most sense to start with streaming.

Real-time insights have value

When designing data science solutions, streaming does not always come to mind first. However, when solutions or tools are built in real time, it is rare that the real-time functionality is not appreciated.

Many analytical solutions of today are built in real time and the tools are available. In many problems, real-time information will be used at some point. Maybe it will not be used from the start, but the day that anomalies happen, you will find a great competitive advantage in having the analytics straight away, rather than waiting till the next hour or the next morning.

Examples of successful implementation of streaming analytics

Let's talk about some examples of companies that have implemented real-time analytics successfully. The first example is Shell. They have been able to implement real-time analytics of their security cameras on their gas stations. An automated and real-time machine learning pipeline is able to detect whether people are smoking.

Another example is the use of sensor data in connected sports equipment. By measuring heart rate and other KPIs in real time, they are able to alert you when anything is wrong with your body.

Of course, the big players such as Facebook and Twitter also analyze a lot of data in real time, for example, when detecting fake news or bad content. There are many successful use cases of streaming analytics, yet at the same time, there are some common challenges that streaming data brings with them. Let's have a look at them now.

Challenges of streaming data

Streaming data analytics are currently less widespread than batch data analytics. Although this is slowly changing, it is good to understand where the challenges are when working with streaming data.

Knowledge of streaming analytics

One simple reason for streaming analytics being less widespread is a question of knowledge and know-how. Setting up streaming analytics is often not taught in schools and is definitely not taught as the go-to method. There are also fewer resources available on the internet to get started with it. As there are much more resources on machine learning and analytics for batch treatment, and the batch methods do not apply to streaming data, people tend to start with batch applications for data science.

Understanding the architecture

A second difficulty when working on streaming data is architecture. Although some data science practitioners have knowledge of architecture, data engineering, and DevOps, this is not always the case. To set up a streaming analytics proof of concept or a **minimum viable product (MVP)**, all those skills are needed. For batch treatment, it is often enough to work with scripts.

Architectural difficulties are inherent to streaming, as it is necessary to work with real-time processes that send individually collected records to an analytical treatment process that will update in real time. If there is no architecture that can handle this, it does not make much sense to start with streaming analytics.

Financial hurdles

Another challenge when working with streaming data is the financial aspect. Although working with streaming is not necessarily more expensive in the long run, it can be more expensive to set up the infrastructure needed to get started. Working on a local developer PC for an MVP is unlikely to succeed as the data needs to be treated in real time.

Risks of runtime problems

Real-time processes also have a larger risk of runtime problems. When building software, bugs and failures happen. If you are on a daily batch process, you may be able to repair the process, rerun the failed batch, and solve the problem.

If a streaming tool is down, there are risks of losing data. As the data should be ingested in real time, the data that is generated during a time-out of your process may not be recuperable. If your process is very important, you will need to set up extensive monitoring day and night and have more quality checks before pushing your solutions to production. Of course, this is also important in batch processes, but even more so in streaming.

Smaller analytics (fewer methods easily available)

The last challenge of streaming analytics is that the common methods are generally developed for batch data first. There are currently many solutions out there for analytics on real time and streaming data, but still not as many as for batch data.

Also, since the streaming analysis has to be done very quickly to respect real-time delivery, streaming use cases tend to end up with much less interesting analytical methodologies and stay at the basic level of descriptive or basic analyses.

How to get started with streaming data

For companies to get started with streaming data, the first step is often to start by putting in place simple applications that **collect real-time data** and make that real-time data accessible in real time. Common use cases to start with are log data, website visits data, or sensor data.

A next step would often be to build **reporting tools** on top of the real-time data source. You can think about KPI dashboards that update in real time, or small and simple alerting tools based on high or low threshold values based on business rules.

When such systems are in place, this leads the way to replace those business rules, or add on top of them. You can think about more advanced analytics tools including real-time **machine learning** for anomaly detection and more.

The most complex step is to add automated feedback loops between your real-time machine learning and your process. After all, there is no reason to stop at **analytics** for business insights if there is potential to automate and improve **decision-making** as well.

Common use cases for streaming data

Let's see a few of the most common use cases for streaming data so that you can get a better feel of the use cases that can benefit from streaming techniques. This will cover three use cases that are relatively accessible for anyone, but of course, there are many more.

Sensor data and anomaly detection

A common use case for streaming data is the analysis of sensor data. Sensor data can occur in a multitude of use cases, such as industry production lines and IoT use cases. When companies decide to collect sensor data, it is often treated in real time.

For a production line, there is great value in detecting anomalies in real time. When too many anomalies occur, the production line can be shut down or the problem can be solved before a number of faulty products are delivered.

A good example of streaming analytics for monitoring humidity for artwork can be found here: `https://azure.github.io/iot-workshop-asset-tracking/step-003-anomaly-detection/`.

Finance and regression forecasting

Finance data is another great use case for streaming data. For example, in the world of stock trading, timing is important. The faster you can detect up or downtrends in the stock market, the faster a trader (or algorithm) can react by selling or buying stocks and making money.

A great example is described in the following paper by K.S Umadevi et al (2018): `https://ieeexplore.ieee.org/document/8554561`.

Clickstream for websites and classification

Websites or apps are a third common use case for real-time insights. If you can track and analyze your visitors in real time, you can propose a personalized experience for them on your website. By proposing products or services that match with a website visitor, you can increase your online sales.

The following paper by Ramanna Hanamanthrao and S Thejaswini (2017) gives a great use case for this technology applied to clickstream data: `https://ieeexplore.ieee.org/abstract/document/8256978`.

Streaming versus big data

It is important to understand different definitions of streaming that you may encounter. One distinction to make is between streaming and big data. Some definitions will consider streaming mainly in a big data (Hadoop/Spark) context, whereas others do not.

Streaming solutions often have a large volume of data, and big data solutions can be the appropriate choice. However, other technologies, combined with a well-chosen hardware architecture, may also be able to do the analytics in real time and, therefore, build streaming solutions without big data technologies.

Streaming versus real-time inference

Real-time inference of models is often built and made accessible via an API. As we define streaming as the analysis of data in real time without batches, such predictions in real time can be considered streaming. You will see more about real-time architectures in a later chapter.

Real-time data formats and importing an example dataset in Python

To finalize this chapter, let's have a look at how to represent streaming data in practice. After all, when building analytics, we will often have to implement test cases and example datasets.

The simplest way to represent streaming data in Python would be to create an iterable object that contains the data and to build your analytics function to work with an iterable.

The following code creates a DataFrame using pandas. There are two columns, temperature and pH:

Code block 1-1

```
import pandas as pd
data_batch = pd.DataFrame({
'temperature': [10, 11, 10, 11, 12, 11, 10, 9, 10, 11, 12, 11,
 9, 12, 11],
    <pH>: [5, 5.5, 6, 5, 4.5, 5, 4.5, 5, 4.5, 5, 4, 4.5, 5,
4.5, 6]
})


print(data_batch)
```

When showing the DataFrame, it will look as follows. The pH is around 4.5/5 but is sometimes higher. The temperature is generally around 10 or 11.

	temperature	pH
0	10	5.0
1	11	5.5
2	10	6.0
3	11	5.0
4	12	4.5
5	11	5.0
6	10	4.5
7	9	5.0
8	10	4.5
9	11	5.0
10	12	4.0
11	11	4.5
12	9	5.0
13	12	4.5
14	11	6.0

Figure 1.5 – The resulting DataFrame

This dataset is a batch dataset; after all, you have all the rows (observations) at the same time. Now, let's see how to convert this dataset to a streaming dataset by making it iterable.

You can do this by iterating through the data's rows. When doing this, you set up a code structure that allows you to add more building blocks to this code one by one. When your developments are done, you will be able to use your code on a real-time stream rather than on an iteration of a DataFrame.

The following code iterates through the rows of the DataFrame and converts the rows to JSON format. This is a very common format for communication between different systems. The JSON of the observation contains a value for temperature and a value for pH. Those are printed out as follows:

Code block 1-2

```
data_iterable = data_batch.iterrows()


for i,new_datapoint in data_iterable:
    print(new_datapoint.to_json())
```

After running this code, you should obtain a print output that looks like the following:

```
{"temperature":10.0,"pH":5.0}
{"temperature":11.0,"pH":5.5}
{"temperature":10.0,"pH":6.0}
{"temperature":11.0,"pH":5.0}
{"temperature":12.0,"pH":4.5}
{"temperature":11.0,"pH":5.0}
{"temperature":10.0,"pH":4.5}
{"temperature":9.0,"pH":5.0}
{"temperature":10.0,"pH":4.5}
{"temperature":11.0,"pH":5.0}
{"temperature":12.0,"pH":4.0}
{"temperature":11.0,"pH":4.5}
{"temperature":9.0,"pH":5.0}
{"temperature":12.0,"pH":4.5}
{"temperature":11.0,"pH":6.0}
```

Figure 1.6 – The resulting print output

Let's now define a super simple example of streaming data analytics. The function that is defined in the following code block will print an alert whenever the temperature gets below 10:

Code block 1-3

```
def super_simple_alert(datapoint):
    if datapoint[<temperature>] < 10:
        print('this is a real time alert. temp too low')
```

You can now add this alert into your simulated streaming process simply by calling the alerting test at every data point. You can use the following code to do this:

Code block 1-4

```
data_iterable = data_batch.iterrows()


for i,new_datapoint in data_iterable:
  print(new_datapoint.to_json())
  super_simple_alert(new_datapoint)
```

When executing this code, you will notice that alerts will be given as soon as the temperature goes below 10:

```
{"temperature":10.0,"pH":5.0}
{"temperature":11.0,"pH":5.5}
{"temperature":10.0,"pH":6.0}
{"temperature":11.0,"pH":5.0}
{"temperature":12.0,"pH":4.5}
{"temperature":11.0,"pH":5.0}
{"temperature":10.0,"pH":4.5}
{"temperature":9.0,"pH":5.0}
this is a real time alert. temp too low
{"temperature":10.0,"pH":4.5}
{"temperature":11.0,"pH":5.0}
{"temperature":12.0,"pH":4.0}
{"temperature":11.0,"pH":4.5}
{"temperature":9.0,"pH":5.0}
this is a real time alert. temp too low
{"temperature":12.0,"pH":4.5}
{"temperature":11.0,"pH":6.0}
```

Figure 1.7 – The resulting print output with alerts on temperature

This alert works only on the temperature, but you could easily add the same type of alert on pH. The following code shows how this can be done. The alert function could be updated to include a second business rule as follows:

Code block 1-5

```
def super_simple_alert(datapoint):
  if datapoint[<temperature>] < 10:
    print('this is a real time alert. temp too low')
```

```
if datapoint[<pH>] > 5.5:
    print('this is a real time alert. pH too high')
```

Executing the function would still be done in exactly the same way:

Code block 1-6

```
data_iterable = data_batch.iterrows()


for i,new_datapoint in data_iterable:
    print(new_datapoint.to_json())
    super_simple_alert(new_datapoint)
```

You will see several alerts being raised throughout the execution on the example streaming data, as follows:

```
{"temperature":10.0,"pH":5.0}
{"temperature":11.0,"pH":5.5}
{"temperature":10.0,"pH":6.0}
this is a real time alert. pH too high
{"temperature":11.0,"pH":5.0}
{"temperature":12.0,"pH":4.5}
{"temperature":11.0,"pH":5.0}
{"temperature":10.0,"pH":4.5}
{"temperature":9.0,"pH":5.0}
this is a real time alert. temp too low
{"temperature":10.0,"pH":4.5}
{"temperature":11.0,"pH":5.0}
{"temperature":12.0,"pH":4.0}
{"temperature":11.0,"pH":4.5}
{"temperature":9.0,"pH":5.0}
this is a real time alert. temp too low
{"temperature":12.0,"pH":4.5}
{"temperature":11.0,"pH":6.0}
this is a real time alert. pH too high
```

Figure 1.8 – The resulting print output with alerts on temperature and pH

With streaming data, you have to decide without seeing the complete data but just on those data points that have been received in the past. This means that there is a need for a different approach to redeveloping algorithms that are similar to batch processing algorithms.

Throughout this book, you will discover methods that apply to streaming data. The difficulty, as you may understand, is that a statistical method is generally developed to compute things using all the data.

Summary

In this introductory chapter on streaming data and streaming analytics, you have first seen some definitions of what streaming data is, and how it is opposed to batch data processing. In streaming data, you need to work with a continuous stream of data, and more traditional (batch) data science solutions need to be adapted to make things work with this newer and more demanding method of data treatment.

You have seen a number of example use cases, and you should now understand that there can be much-added value for businesses and advanced technology use cases to have data science and analytics calculated on the fly rather than wait for a fixed moment. Real-time insights can be a game-changer, and autonomous machine learning solutions often need real-time decision capabilities.

You have seen an example in which a data stream was created and a simple real-time alerting system was developed. In the next chapter, you will get a much deeper introduction to a number of streaming solutions. In practice, data scientists and analysts will generally not be responsible for putting streaming data ingestion in place, but they will be constrained by the limits of those systems. It is, therefore, important to have a good understanding of streaming and real-time architecture: this will be the goal of the next chapter.

Further reading

- *What is streaming data?* (by AWS): `https://aws.amazon.com/streaming-data/`

- *The 8 Best Examples of Real-Time Data Analytics*, by Bernard Marr: `https://www.linkedin.com/pulse/8-best-examples-real-time-data-analytics-bernard-marr/`

- *How to Build a Strong Business Case For Streaming Analytics*, Forbes `https://www.forbes.com/sites/forbestechcouncil/2021/10/26/how-to-build-a-strong-business-case-for-streaming-analytics/?sh=314e2b8a465d`

- *7 enterprise use cases for real-time streaming analytics*: `https://searchbusinessanalytics.techtarget.com/feature/7-enterprise-use-cases-for-real-time-streaming-analytics`

- *From batch to online/stream*, by RiverML: `https://riverml.xyz/dev/examples/batch-to-online/`

- Anaconda: `https://www.anaconda.com/products/individual`

- Google Colab: `https://colab.research.google.com/`

- Kaggle Notebooks: `https://www.kaggle.com/code`

2

Architectures for Streaming and Real-Time Machine Learning

Streaming architectures are an essential component of solutions for real-time machine learning and streaming analytics. Even if you have a model or other analytics tools that can treat data in real time, update, and respond straight away, this will be of no use if there is no architecture to support your solution.

The first important consideration is making sure that your models and analytics can function on each data point; there needs to be an update function and/or a predict function that can update the solution on each new observation being received by the system.

Another important consideration for real-time and streaming architectures is data ingress: how to make sure that data can be received on an observation per observation basis, rather than the more traditional batch approach with daily database updates, for example.

Besides that, it will be important that you understand how to make different software systems communicate. For example, data has to flow very fast from your data generating process, maybe go through a data storage solution, a data quality tool, or a security layer, and then be received by your analytics program. The analytics program will do its work and send the result back to the source, or maybe forward the treated data points to a visualization solution, an alerting system, or similar.

In this chapter, you will get an introduction to architectures for streaming and real-time machine learning. The central focus of this book will remain on the analytics and machine learning part of the pipeline. The goal of this chapter is to give you enough elements to imagine and implement rough working architectures, while some of the highly-specialized parts on performance, availability, and security will be left out.

This chapter covers the following topics:

1. Defining your analytics as a function
2. Understanding microservices architecture
3. Communicating between services through APIs
4. Demystifying the HTTP protocol
5. Building a simple API on AWS
6. Big data tools for real-time streaming
7. Calling a big data environment in real time

Technical requirements

You can find all the code for this book on GitHub at the following link: `https://github.com/PacktPublishing/Machine-Learning-for-Streaming-Data-with-Python`. If you are not yet familiar with Git and GitHub, the easiest way to download the notebooks and code samples is the following:

1. Go to the link of the repository.
2. Go to the green **Code** button.
3. Select **Download ZIP**.

When you download the ZIP file, you unzip it in your local environment, and you will be able to access the code through your preferred Python editor.

Python environment

To follow along with this book, you can download the code in the repository and execute it using your preferred Python editor.

If you are not yet familiar with Python environments, I would advise you to check out Anaconda (`https://www.anaconda.com/products/individual`), which comes with the Jupyter Notebook and JupyterLab, which are both great for executing notebooks. It also comes with Spyder and VSCode for editing scripts and programs.

If you have difficulty installing Python or the associated programs on your machine, you can check out Google Colab (`https://colab.research.google.com/`) or Kaggle Notebooks (`https://www.kaggle.com/code`), which both allow you to run Python code in online notebooks for free, without any setup to do.

> **Note**
> The code in the book will generally use Colab and Kaggle Notebooks with Python version 3.7.13, and you can set up your own environment to mimic this.

Defining your analytics as a function

In order to get started with architecture, let's build an idea from the ground up using the different building blocks that are necessary to make this a minimal working product.

The first thing that you need to have for this is an understanding of the type of real-time analytics that you want to execute.

For now, let's go with the same example as in the previous chapter: a real-time business rule that prints an alert when the temperature or acidity of our production line is out of the acceptable limits.

In the previous chapter, this alert was coded as follows:

Code block 2-1

```python
def super_simple_alert(datapoint):
    if datapoint['temperature'] < 10:
        print('this is a real time alert. temp too low')
    if datapoint['pH'] > 5.5:
        print('this is a real time alert. pH too high')
```

In the previous chapter, you used an iteration over a DataFrame to test out this code. In reality, you will always need an idea of architecture so that you can make your code actually receive data in real time from a data generating process. This building block will be covered in this chapter.

In the following schematic drawing, you see a high-level architectural schema for our streaming solution:

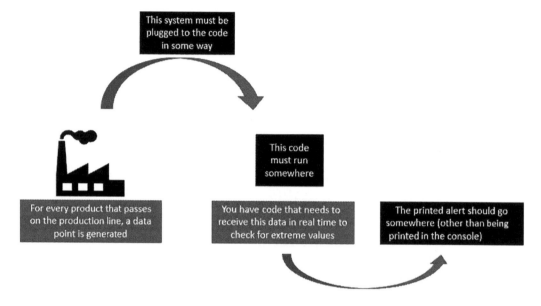

Figure 2.1 – A high-level architectural schema for a streaming solution

In this schematic drawing, you clearly see that writing code will give you some of the key components of your solution. However, you need to build an architecture around this to make the solution come to life. The darker pieces are still missing from the example implementation.

While the goal of this book is not to give a full in-depth course on architecture, you will discover some tools and building blocks here that will allow you to deliver an MVP real-time use case. To get your building blocks cleanly organized, you will need to choose an architectural structure for your solutions. Microservices are an architectural pattern that will allow you to build clean, small building blocks and have them communicate with each other.

Understanding microservices architecture

The concept of **microservices** is important to understand when working on architectures. Although there are other ways to architecture software projects, microservices are quite popular for a good reason. They help teams be flexible and effective, and help to keep software flexible and clearly structured.

The idea behind microservices is in the name: software is represented as many small services that operate individually. When looking at the overall architecture, each of the microservices is inside a small, *black box* with clearly defined inputs and outputs. Processes are put in place to call the right black box at the right time.

Microservice architecture is loosely coupled. This means that there is no fixed communication between the different microservices. Instead, each microservice can be called, or not called, by any other services or code.

If a change needs to be made to one of the microservices, the scope of the change is fairly local, thereby not affecting other microservices. As input and output are predefined, this also helps in keeping the foundational structure of the program in order, without it being fixed in any way.

To allow different microservices to communicate, an often-chosen solution is to use **Application Programming Interfaces** (**APIs**). Let's deep dive into those now.

Communicating between services through APIs

A central component in microservice architectures is the use of APIs. An API is a part that allows you to connect two microservices (or other pieces of code) together.

APIs are much like websites. Just like a website, an API is built behind a website-like link or an IP address. When you go to a website, the server of the website sends you the code that represents the website. Your internet browser then interprets this code and shows you a web page.

When you call an API, the API will receive your request. The request triggers your code to be run on the server and generates a response that is sent back to you. If something goes wrong (maybe your request was not as expected or an error occurs), you may not receive any response, or receive an error code such as `request not authorized` or `internal server error`.

The following figure shows a flow chart that covers this. A computer or user sends an HTTP request, and the API server sends back the response according to the code that runs on the API server:

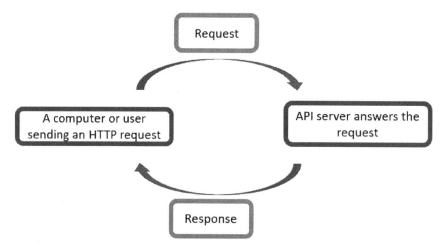

Figure 2.2 – A high-level architectural schema for a streaming solution

You can call APIs with a lot of different tools. Sometimes, you can even use your internet browser, otherwise, tools such as cURL do the job on the command line. You can use tools such as Postman or Insomnia for calling APIs with a user interface. All the communication is covered in fixed rules and practices, which, together, are called the HTTP protocol, which we will explore in the next section.

Demystifying the HTTP protocol

Interaction between services (or websites) uses the HTTP protocol. When working with APIs and building communicating microservices, it is important to understand the basics of the HTTP protocol.

The most important thing to know is how to send and format requests and responses.

The GET request

The simplest HTTP request is the GET request. You use this when you need to get something from a server or a service. For example, when going to a website, your browser sends a GET request to the website's IP address to obtain the website's layout code.

A GET request can simply be sent from Python using the following code:

Code block 2-2

```
import requests
import json
response = requests.get('http://www.google.com')
print(response.status_code)
print(response.text)
```

This code uses the requests library in Python to send a GET request to the Google home page. This is technically the same process as going to your internet browser and going to the Google home page. You'll obtain all the code that is needed for your web browser to show you the Google home page. Although many of you are very familiar with the look of the Google home page in your browser, it is much less recognizable in this code response. It is important to understand that it is actually exactly the same thing, just in a different format.

The POST request

The POST request is another request that you'll encounter very often. It allows you to send some data with your request. This is often necessary, especially in analytics APIs, as the analytics are likely to happen on this data. By adding the data in the body of the POST request, you make sure that your analytics code received your data.

The syntax in Python will be something like the following code block. For now, this code doesn't work as you have not built a server that is able to do something with this data. However, just keep in mind that the POST request allows you to send your data point to an API with the goal of obtaining a response:

Code block 2-3

```
import requests
import json
data = {'temperature': 10, 'pH': 5.5}

response = requests.post('http://www.example.com',data=data)

print(response.status_code)
print(response.text)
```

JSON format for communication between systems

The most common format for interaction between services is the **JavaScript Object Notation (JSON)** format. It is a data type that very strongly resembles the dictionary format in Python. In effect, it is a key-value object that is surrounded by accolades.

An example of a JSON payload is as follows:

Code block 2-4

```
{
    'name': 'your name',
    'address': 'your address',
    'age': 'your age'
}
```

This data format is fairly easy to understand and very commonly used. It is, therefore, important to understand how it works. You'll see its use later on in the chapter as well.

RESTful APIs

While API development is out of scope for this book, it will be useful to have some pointers and best practices. The most used API structure is the **Representational State Transfer (REST)** API.

The REST API works just like other APIs, but it follows a certain set of style rules that make it recognizable as a REST API, also called the RESTful API.

There are six guiding constraints in REST APIs:

- Client-server architecture
- Statelessness
- Cacheability
- Layered system
- Code on demand (optional)
- Uniform interface

If you want to go further on this, some further reading resources are provided at the end of the chapter. Now that we have learned about the HTTP protocol, let's build an API on **Amazon Web Services (AWS)**.

Building a simple API on AWS

In order to do something practical, let's build a super simple API on AWS. This will allow you to understand how different services can communicate together. It can also serve as a good testing environment for putting the examples in the rest of the book to the test.

You will use the following components of the AWS framework.

API Gateway in AWS

This is an AWS service that handles API requests for you. You specify the type of request that you expect to receive, and you specify the action that should be taken upon reception of a request. When building an API using API Gateway, this will automatically generate an IP address or link to which you can send your API requests.

Lambda in AWS

Lambda is a serverless execution environment for code. This means that you can write Python code, plug it to the API Gateway, and not think about how to set up servers, firewalls, and all that. This is great for decoupling systems, and it is fast enough for many real-time systems.

Data-generating process on a local machine

As the last component, you will build a separate data-generating process in Python. You can execute this code in a notebook. Every time a new data point is generated, the code will call the API with the analytics service and reply with an alert if needed.

A schematic overview of this architecture can be seen in the following figure:

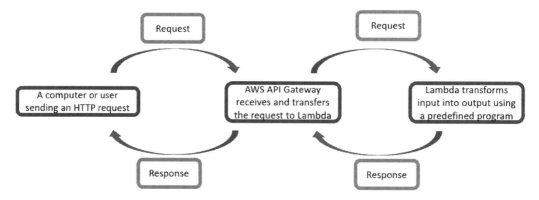

Figure 2.3 – Detailed architecture schema for AWS

Implementing the example

In order to implement the example, we will use the following step-by-step instructions. If you have an AWS account, you can skip *Step 0*.

Step 0 – Creating an account on AWS

If you do not yet have an account on AWS, it is easy to create one. You will have to set it up with a credit card, but the services that we will use here all have a free tier. As long as you shut down the resources at the end of your test, you are unlikely to incur any fees. However, be careful, because mistakes happen, and if you use a lot of resources on AWS, you will end up paying.

To set up an account, you can simply follow the steps on `aws.amazon.com`.

Step 1 – Setting up a Lambda function

Upon receipt of the `POST` request, a Lambda function has to be called to execute our alert and send back the response.

Go to **Lambda** in the **Services** menu and click on **Create function**. You will see the following screen:

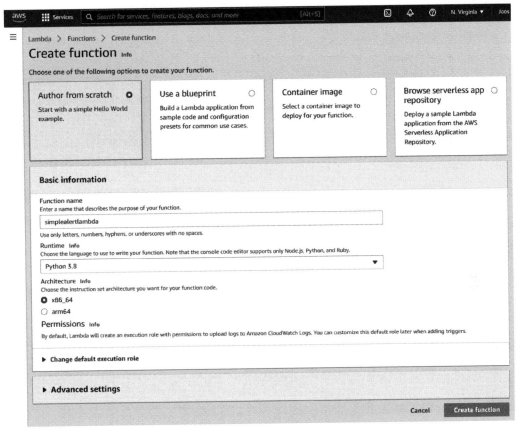

Figure 2.4 – Creating a Lambda function

Make sure to select **Python** and to give the appropriate name to your function.

When you have finished creating the function, it is time to code it. You can use the following code for this:

Code block 2-5

```python
import json
def super_simple_alert(datapoint):
    answer = ''
    if datapoint['temperature'] < 10:
        answer += 'temp too low '
    if datapoint['pH'] > 5.5:
        answer += 'pH too high '
    if answer == '':
```

```
        answer = 'all good'
    return answer
def lambda_handler(event, context):
    answer = super_simple_alert(event)
    return {
        'statusCode': 200,
        'body': json.dumps({'status': answer}),
    }
```

This code has two functions. The `super_simple_alert` function takes a `datapoint` and returns an answer (an alarm in string format). The `lambda_handler` function is the code that deals with the incoming API calls. The event contains the `datapoint`, so the event is passed to the `super_simple_alert` function in order to analyze whether an alert should be launched. This is stored in the `answer` variable. Finally, the `lambda_handler` function returns a Python dictionary with the status code `200` and a body that contains the answer.

The window should now look as follows:

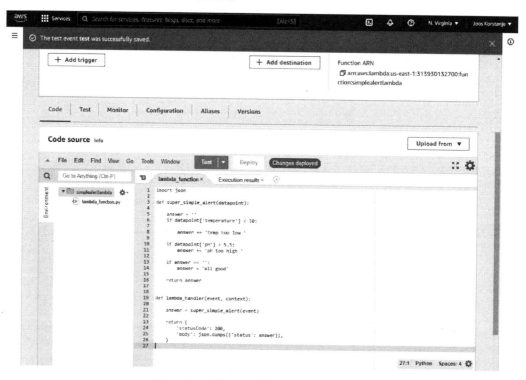

Figure 2.5 – The Lambda function window

Step 2 – Set up API Gateway

As a first step, let's set up API Gateway to receive a POST request. The POST request will contain a body in which there is JSON that has a value for temperature and pH, just like in the alerting example.

To set up API Gateway, you have to go to the **API Gateway** menu, which is accessible through the **Services** menu. The **Management** console looks as follows:

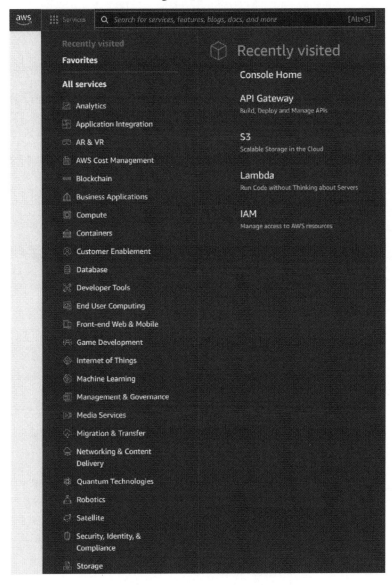

Figure 2.6 – The AWS Management console

You should end up on the **API Gateway** menu, which looks as follows:

Figure 2.7 – The API Gateway menu

When you are in the **API Gateway** menu, you can go to **Create API** to set up your first API.

Inside **Create API**, do the following steps:

1. Select **REST API**.

2. Choose the **REST** protocol.

3. Build the API as a new API.

4. Create an API name, for example, `streamingAPI`.

You will obtain an empty API configuration menu, as follows:

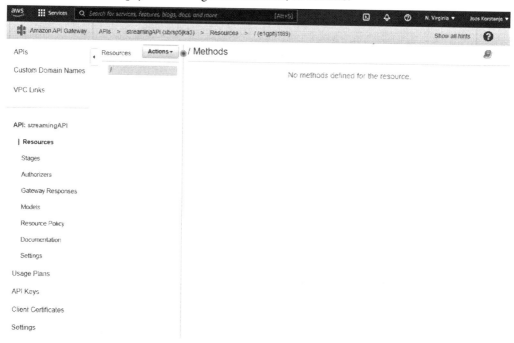

Figure 2.8 – Adding a method in API Gateway

We want to add a POST method, so go to **Actions | Create Method**. Select **POST** in the dropdown and click on the small **v** character next to the word **POST** to create the POST method. The following menu will appear for setting up the POST method:

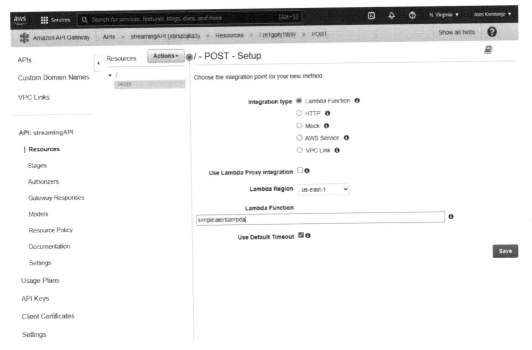

Figure 2.9 – The POST setup

Step 3 – Deploy the API

Still in the API Gateway menu, click on **Actions | Deploy API.** You can create a new stage called `test` to deploy to. You can use the default setup for this stage, but it is important to take the URL that is on top here to be able to call your API from your data generation process. You will need to set the settings as shown in the following screenshot:

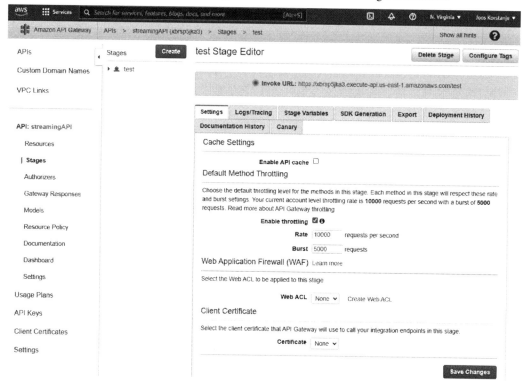

Figure 2.10 – More details for the API

Step 4 – Calling your API from another Python environment

Now, you can call your API from another Python environment, such as a notebook on your own computer, or from a Google Colab notebook.

You can use the following code to do that:

Code block 2-6

```
import requests
import json
data = {'temperature': 8, 'pH': 4}
```

```
response = requests.post('YOUR_URL', data = json.dumps(data))
print(json.loads(response.text))
```

You will obtain the following answer:

Code block 2-7

```
{'statusCode': 200, 'body': '{"status": "temp too low "}'}
```

Now, you can imagine how a real-time data-generating process would simply call the API at each new data point and alerts would be generated right away!

More architectural considerations

Although this is a great first try at building an API, you should be aware that there is much more to think about when you want to build this in a reliable and secure way. There is a reason that data science and software engineering are different jobs, and it takes time to learn all the skills necessary to manage an API from A to Z. In general, this will not be asked of a data scientist.

Some of the things that were not covered in this example are as follows:

- Performance: scaling, load balancing, and latency
- DDoS attacks
- Security and hacking
- Financial aspects of API invocation
- Dependency on a cloud provider versus being cloud provider agnostic

At the end of the chapter, there are some resources for further reading, which you can check out.

Other AWS services and other services in general that have the same functionality

The current example used API Gateway and a Lambda function to build an API. The advantages of this method are the easiness of access and setup, which makes it great as a method to present in this book. However, you should be aware that there are many other tools and technologies for building APIs.

AWS is one of the most used cloud providers, and most things that can be done on AWS can be done on the other cloud providers' platforms as well. Examples of other big players are Google's GCP and Microsoft's Azure. Even on AWS, there are many alternatives.

You can also build APIs in local environments. When doing this, you'll again have a large choice of tools and providers. Now that you have seen how to build an API using standard programming in Python and using a microservices approach, you will next see some alternatives using the big data environment. Big data environments generally have a steeper learning curve and may often be made for a specific use case, but they can be very powerful and absolutely necessary when working with high volume and velocity.

Big data tools for real time streaming

There are many big data tools that do real-time streaming analytics. They can be great alternatives for *regular* real-time systems, especially when volumes are large and high speeds are required.

As a reminder, the term **big data** is generally used to regroup tools that solve problems that are too complex to fit in memory The problems solved have three core characteristics: volume, variety, and velocity.

Big data tools are generally known for doing a lot of work in parallel computing. When writing non-optimized, regular Python code, the code will often pass data points one by one. Big data solutions solve this by treating data points in parallel on multiple servers. This approach makes big data tools faster whenever there is a lot of data, but slower when there is little data (due to the overhead of managing the different workers).

Big data tools are often relatively specific; they should only be used for use cases that have vast amounts of data. It does not make sense to start working on big data tools for every problem at hand.

Numerous such solutions are made for working with streaming data. Let's have a look at some commonly used tools:

- **Spark Streaming**: Spark Streaming is an addition to Spark, one of the main tools for big data nowadays. Spark Streaming can be plugged into sources such as Kafka, Flume, and Amazon Kinesis, thereby making streaming data accessible in a Spark environment.

- **Apache Kafka**: Kafka is an open source tool managed by Apache. It is a framework that is made for delivering real-time data feeds. It is used by many companies to deliver data pipelines and streaming analytics. Even some cloud providers have integrated Kafka into their solutions.

- **Apache Flume**: Apache Flume is another open source tool managed by Apache, which also focuses on streaming data. Flume is specifically used for treating large amounts of log data in a big data environment.

- **Apache Beam**: Another tool in the Apache streaming family is Apache Beam. This tool can handle both batch and streaming data. It is best known for building ETL and data processing pipelines.

- **Apache Storm**: Apache Storm is a stream processing computation framework that allows doing distributed computation. It is used to process data streams with Hadoop in real time.

- **Apache NiFi**: Apache NiFi is a tool that focuses on ETL. It gives its users the possibility to automate and manage data flows between systems. It can work together with Kafka.

- **Google Cloud DataFlow**: Google Cloud DataFlow is a tool proposed by Google Cloud Platform. It is developed specifically for tackling streaming use cases. It allows users to execute Apache Beam pipelines in a fully managed service.

- **Amazon Kinesis**: Amazon Kinesis is strongly based on open source Apache Kafka, which was discussed earlier. The advantage of using Kinesis over Kafka is that it comes with a lot of things that are managed for you, whereas if you use Kafka directly, you spend more effort on managing the service. Of course, in return, you must use the AWS platform to access it.

- **Azure Stream Analytics**: Azure Stream Analytics is the main streaming analytics service proposed on Microsoft's cloud platform, Azure. It is a real-time analytics service that is based on Trill.

- **IBM Streams**: IBM Streams is a streaming analytics tool that is proposed on the IBM cloud. Just like Kinesis, it is based on the open source Kafka project.

Calling a big data environment in real time

If your real-time analytics service is managed by a big data or specific streaming tool, you cannot always follow the API method for connecting your real-time process to your analytics process.

In most cases, you'll need to look into the documentation of the tool of your choice and make sure that you understand how to make the connections work. At this point, you are often going to need a specialized profile to work with you, as this level of architecture and data engineering is generally considered out of scope for most data scientists.

A general difference between the microservice system and the big data system is that in a microservice approach, we are generally considering that there must be a response coming from the API that is taken into account by the calling service.

In big data environments, it is much more common for a service such as a website to send data to a big data environment but not need a response. You could imagine a website that writes out every interaction by a user to a fixed location as JSON files. The big data streaming tool is then plugged onto this data storage location to read in the data in a streaming fashion and converts this into an analysis, a visualization, or something else.

Let's build a minimal example that will show how to do this:

1. First, create a JSON file called `example.json`, in which you write only the following data:

Code block 2-8

```
{'value':'hello'}
```

2. You can now write a very short piece of Spark Streaming code that reads this data in a streaming way:

```
from pyspark.sql import SparkSession
from pyspark.sql.types import *

spark = SparkSession \
    .builder \
    .appName("quickexample") \
    .getOrCreate()

schema = StructType([ StructField("value", String-
Type(), True) ])

streamingDF = (
  spark
    .readStream
    .schema(schema)
    .json('example.json')
)

display(streamingDF)
```

In short, this code starts by creating a `spark` session. Once the session is created, a schema is defined for the `example.json` file. As it has only one key (called `value`), the schema is quite short. The data type for the value is `string`.

You then see that the data is imported using the `.readStream` method, which actually does a lot of the heavy lifting in streaming for you. If you'd like to go further with this example, you could write all kinds of analytical Spark functions using the `streamingDF` library and you will have streaming analytics using the well-known big data tool **PySpark**.

Summary

In this chapter, you have started to discover the field of architecture. You have built your own API on AWS, and you have seen the basic foundation of communication between systems. You should now understand that data is key in communication between systems and that good communication between systems is essential for delivering value through analytics.

This is especially true in the case of real-time and streaming analytics. The high speed and often large size of data can easily pose problems if architectural bottlenecks are not identified early enough in the project.

There are other topics that you must remember to take into account, including security, availability, and compliance. Those topics are best left to someone who makes it their full-time responsibility to take care of such data architecture problems.

In the following chapter, we'll go back to the core of this book, as you'll discover how to build analytics use cases on streaming data.

Further reading

- *Microservices Architecture*: https://cloud.google.com/learn/what-is-microservices-architecture

- API: https://www.redhat.com/en/topics/api/what-are-application-programming-interfaces

- HTTP: https://developer.mozilla.org/en-US/docs/Web/HTTP

- *Top 10 real-time data streaming tools*: https://ipspecialist.net/top-10-real-time-data-streaming-tools/

- Spark Streaming: https://spark.apache.org/docs/latest/streaming-programming-guide.html

- Kafka: https://kafka.apache.org/

- Flume: `https://flume.apache.org/`

- Beam: `https://beam.apache.org/`

- Storm: `https://storm.apache.org/`

- NiFi: `https://nifi.apache.org/`

- Google Cloud Dataflow: `https://cloud.google.com/dataflow`

- Amazon Kinesis: `https://aws.amazon.com/kinesis/`

- Azure Stream Analytics: `https://azure.microsoft.com/en-us/services/stream-analytics/`

- IBM Streams: `https://www.ibm.com/docs/en/streams`

- *Capturing Web Page Scroll Progress with Amazon Kinesis*, by AWS: `https://docs.aws.amazon.com/sdk-for-javascript/v2/developer-guide/kinesis-examples-capturing-page-scrolling.html`

3
Data Analysis on Streaming Data

Now that you have seen an introduction to streaming data and streaming use cases, as well as an introduction to streaming architecture, it is time to enter into the core of this book: analytics and machine learning.

As you probably know, descriptive statistics and data analysis are the entry points into machine learning, but they are also often used as a standalone use case. In this chapter, you will first discover descriptive statistics from a traditional statistics viewpoint. Some parts of traditional statistics focus on making correct estimations of descriptive statistics when only part of the data is available.

In streaming, you will encounter such problems in an even more impacting manner than in batch data. Through a continuous data collection process, your descriptive statistics will continue changing on every new data point. This chapter will propose some solutions for dealing with this.

You will also build a data visualization based on those descriptive statistics. After all, the human brain is wired in such a way that visual presentations are much easier to read than data matrices. Data visualization is an important tool to master and comes with some additional reflections to take into account when working on streaming data.

The chapter will conclude with a short introduction to statistical process control. This subdomain of statistics focuses on analyzing a continuous stream of measurements. Although streaming analytics was not yet a thing when process control was invented, it became a new, important use case for those analytical methods.

This chapter covers the following topics:

- Descriptive statistics on streaming data
- Introduction to sampling theory
- Overview of the main descriptive statistics
- Real-time visualizations
- Basic alerting systems

Technical requirements

You can find all the code for this book on GitHub at the following link: `https://github.com/PacktPublishing/Machine-Learning-for-Streaming-Data-with-Python`. If you are not yet familiar with Git and GitHub, the easiest way to download the notebooks and code samples is the following:

1. Go to the link of the repository.
2. Click the green **Code** button.
3. Select **Download ZIP**.

When you download the ZIP file, unzip it in your local environment and you will be able to access the code through your preferred Python editor.

Python environment

To follow along with this book, you can download the code in the repository and execute it using your preferred Python editor.

If you are not yet familiar with Python environments, I would advise you to check out Anaconda (`https://www.anaconda.com/products/individual`), which comes with Jupyter Notebook and JupyterLab, which are both great for executing notebooks. It also comes with Spyder and VSCode for editing scripts and programs.

If you have difficulty installing Python or the associated programs on your machine, you can check out Google Colab (`https://colab.research.google.com/`) or Kaggle Notebooks (`https://www.kaggle.com/code`), which both allow you to run Python code in online notebooks for free, without any setup to do.

> **Note**
>
> The code in the book will generally use Colab and Kaggle Notebooks with Python version 3.7.13 and you can set up your own environment to mimic this.

Descriptive statistics on streaming data

Computing descriptive statistics is generally one of the first things covered in statistics and data analytics courses. Descriptive statistics are measurements that data practitioners are very familiar with, as they allow you to summarize a dataset in a small set of indicators.

Why are descriptive statistics different on streaming data?

On regular datasets, you can use almost any statistical software to easily obtain descriptive statistics using well-known formulas. On streaming datasets, unfortunately, this is much less obvious.

The problem with applying descriptive statistics on streaming data is that the formulas are made for finding fixed measurements. In streaming data, you continue to receive new data, which unfortunately may alter your values. When you do not have all the data of a variable, you cannot be certain about its value. In the following section, you will get an introduction to sampling theory, the domain that deals with estimating parameters from data samples.

Introduction to sampling theory

Before diving into descriptive statistics in streaming data, it is important to understand the basics of descriptive statistics in regular data. The domain that deals with the estimation of descriptive statistics using samples of the data is called **sampling theory**.

Comparing population and sample

In regular statistics, the concept of population and sample is very important. Let's have a look at the definitions before diving into it further:

- **Individual**: Individuals are the individual objects or people that are included in a study. If your study looks at products on a production line and you measure the characteristics of a product, then the individual is the product. If you are doing a study on website sales and you track data on each website visitor, then your individual is the website visitor.

- **Population**: A statistical population is generally defined as the pool of individuals from which a sample is drawn. The population contains any individual that would theoretically qualify to participate in a study. In the production line example, the population would be all the products. In the website example, the population would be all the website visitors.

- **Sample**: A sample is defined as a subset of the population on which you are going to execute your study. In most statistical studies, you work with a sample; you do not have data on all possible individuals in the world, but rather, you have a subset, which you hope is large enough. There are numerous statistical tools that help you to decide whether this is the case.

Population parameters and sample statistics

When computing descriptive statistics on a sample, they are called **sample statistics**. Sample statistics are based on a sample, and although they are generally reliable estimates of the population, they are not perfect about the population.

For the population, the term used is **population parameters**. They are accurate, and there is no measurement error here. However, they are, in most cases, impossible to measure, as you'll never have enough time and money to measure every individual in the population.

Sample statistics allow you to estimate population parameters.

Sampling distribution

The sampling distribution is the distribution of the statistics. Imagine that a population of website customers spends, on average, 300 seconds (5 minutes) on your website. If you were drawing 100 random samples of your website visitors, and you computed the mean of each of those samples, you'd probably end up with 100 different estimates.

The distribution of those estimates is called the **sampling distribution**. It will follow a normal distribution in which the mean should be relatively close to the population mean. The standard deviation of the sampling distribution is called the **standard error**. The standard error is used to estimate the stability or representativeness of your samples.

Sample size calculations and confidence level

In traditional statistics, sample size calculations can be used to define the number of elements that you need to have in a sample for the sample to be reliable. You need to define a confidence level and a sample size calculation formula for your specific statistic. Together, they will allow you to identify the sample size needed for reliably estimating your population parameters using sample statistics.

Rolling descriptive statistics from streaming

In streaming analytics, you will have more and more data as time goes on. It would be possible to recompute the overall statistics at the reception of a new data point. At some point, new data points will have very little impact compared to a large number of data points in the past. If a change occurs in the stream, it will take time for this change to be reflected in the descriptive statistic, and this is, therefore, not generally the best approach.

The general approach for descriptive statistics on streaming data is to use a rolling window for computing and recomputing the descriptive statistics. Once you have decided on a definition of your window, you compute the statistics for all observations that are in your window.

An example can be to choose a window of the last 25 products. This way, every time a new product measurement comes into your analytical application, you compute the average of this product together with the 24 preceding products.

The more observations you have in your window, the less impact your last observation has. This can be great if you want to avoid false alarms, but it can be dangerous if you need every single product to be perfect. Choosing small numbers of individuals in your window will make your descriptive statistics vary heavily if a variation is present in your descriptive statistics.

Tuning the window period is a good exercise to do when trying to fine-tune your descriptive statistics. By trying out different approaches, you can find the method that works best for your use case.

Exponential weight

Another tool that you can use for fine-tuning your descriptive statistics on streaming data is exponential weighting. Exponential weighting puts exponentially more weight on recent observations and less on past observations. This allows you to take in more historical observations without affecting the importance of recent observations.

Tracking convergence as an additional KPI

When tracking descriptive statistics on a stream of data, it is a possibility to report multiple time windows of your measurements. For example, you could build a dashboard that informs your clients of the averages of the day, but at the same time, you can report the averages of the last hour and the averages of the last 15 minutes.

By doing this, you may, for example, give your client the information that the day and hour went well in general (day and hour averages are according to specification), but in the last 15 minutes, your product starts to present problems, and the last 15 minutes' average is not according to specification. With this information, the operators can intervene quickly and stop or change the process according to their needs, without having to worry about the production earlier on in the day.

Overview of the main descriptive statistics

Let's now have a look at the most used descriptive statistics and see how you can adapt them to use a rolling window on any data stream. Of course, as you have seen in the previous chapter, streaming analytics can be executed on a multitude of tools. The important takeaway is to understand which descriptive analytics to use and to have a basis that can be adapted to different streaming input tools.

The mean

The first descriptive statistic that will be covered is the mean. The mean is the most commonly used measure of centrality.

Interpretation and use

Together with other measures of centrality, such as the median and the mode, its goal is to describe the center of the distribution of a variable. If the distribution is perfectly symmetrical, the mean, median, and mode will be equal. If there is a skewed distribution, the mean will be affected by the outliers and move in the direction of the skew or the outliers.

Formula

The formula for the sample mean is the following:

$$\bar{x} = \frac{\sum_{i=1}^{n} x_i}{n}$$

In this formula, n is the sample size and x is the value of the variable in the sample.

Code

There are many Python functions that you can use for the mean. One of those is the numpy function called mean. You can see an example of it used here:

Code block 3-1

```
values = [10,8,12,11,7,10,8,9,12,11,10]
import numpy as np
np.mean(values)
```

You should obtain a result of 9.8181.

The median

The median is the second measure of the centrality of a variable or a distribution.

Interpretation and use

Like the mean, the median is used to indicate the center. However, a difference from the mean is that the median is not sensitive to outliers and is much less sensitive to skewed distributions.

An example where this is important is when studying the salaries of a country's population. Salaries are known to follow a strongly skewed distribution. Most people make between a minimum wage and an average wage. Few people make very high amounts of money. When computing the mean, it will be too high to represent the overall population, as it gets boosted upward by the high earners. Using the median is more sensible as it will more closely represent a lot of people.

The median represents the point where 50% of the people will earn less than this amount and 50% will earn more than this amount.

Formula

The formula for the median is relatively complex to read, as it does not work with the actual values, but rather, it takes the middle value after ordering all the values from low to high. If there is an even number of values, there is no middle, so it will take the average of the two middle values:

$$median(x) = \begin{cases} x\left[\dfrac{n+1}{2}\right] & \text{if } n \text{ is odd} \\ \dfrac{x\left[\dfrac{n}{2}\right] + x\left[\dfrac{n}{2}+1\right]}{2} & \text{if } n \text{ is even} \end{cases}$$

Here, x is an ordered list and the brackets indicate indexing on this list.

Code

You can compute the median as follows:

Code block 3-2

```
values = [10,8,12,11,7,10,8,9,12,11,10]

import numpy as np
np.median(values)
```

The result of this computation should be 10.

The mode

The mode is the third commonly used measure of centrality in descriptive statistics. This section will explain its use and implementation in Python.

Interpretation and use

The mode represents the value that was present the most often in the data. If you have a continuous (numeric) variable, then you generally create bins to regroup your data before computing the mode. This way, you can make sure that it is representative.

Formula

The easiest way to find the mode is to count the number of occurrences per group or per value and take the value with the highest occurrences as the mode. This will work for categorical as well as numerical variables.

Code

You can use the following code to find the mode in Python:

Code block 3-3

```
values = [10,8,12,11,7,10,8,9,12,11,10]

import statistics
statistics.mode(values)
```

The obtained result should be 10.

Standard deviation

You will now see a number of descriptive statistics for variability, starting with the standard deviation.

Interpretation and use

The standard deviation is a commonly used measure for variability. Measures for variability show the spread around the center that is present in your data. For example, where the mean can indicate the average salary of your population, it does not tell you whether everyone is close to this value or whether everyone is very far away. Measures of variability allow you to obtain this information.

Formula

The sample standard deviation can be computed as follows:

$$s = \sqrt{\frac{\sum_{i=1}^{n}(x_i - \bar{x})^2}{n - 1}}$$

Code

You can compute the sample standard deviation as follows:

Code block 3-4

```
values = [10,8,12,11,7,10,8,9,12,11,10]

import numpy as np
np.std(values, ddof=1)
```

You should obtain a result of 1.66.

Variance

The variance is another measure of variability, and it is closely related to the standard deviation. Let's see how it works.

Interpretation and use

The variance is simply the square of the standard deviation. It is sometimes easier to work with the formula of variance, as it does not involve taking the square root. It is, therefore, easier to handle in some mathematical operations. The standard deviation is generally easier to use for interpretation.

Formula

The formula for variance is the following:

$$s^2 = \frac{\sum_{i=1}^{n}(x_i - \bar{x})^2}{n-1}$$

Code

You can use the following code for computing the sample variance:

Code block 3-5

```
values = [10,8,12,11,7,10,8,9,12,11,10]

import numpy as np
np.var(values, ddof=1)
```

The obtained result should be 2.76.

Quartiles and interquartile range

The third measure of variability that will be covered is the **interquartile range (IQR)**. This will conclude the statistics for describing variability.

Interpretation and use

The IQR is a measure that is related to the median in some way. If you remember, the median is the point where 50% of the values are lower than it and 50% of the values are higher; it is really a middle point.

The same can be done with a 25/75% split instead of a 50/50% split. In that case, they are called quartiles. By computing the first quartile (25% is lower and 75% is higher) and the third quartile (75% is lower and 25% is higher), you can get an idea of the variability of your data as well. The difference between the third quartile and the first quartile is called the IQR.

Formula

The formula for the IQR is simply the difference between the third and first quartiles, as follows:

$$IQR = Q3 - Q1$$

Code

You can use the following Python code to compute the IQR:

Code block 3-6

```
values = [10,8,12,11,7,10,8,9,12,11,10]

import scipy.stats
scipy.stats.iqr(values)
```

You should find an IQR of 2.5.

Correlations

Correlation is a descriptive statistic for describing relations hips between multiple variables. Let's see how it works.

Interpretation and use

Now that you have seen multiple measures of centrality and variability, you will now discover a descriptive statistic that allows you to study relations hips between two variables. The main descriptive statistic for this is **correlation**. There are multiple formulas and definitions of correlation, but here, you will see the most common one: Pearson correlation.

The correlation coefficient will be -1 for strong negative correlation, 1 for strong positive correlation, 0 for no correlation, or somewhere in between.

Formula

The formula for Pearson's correlation coefficient is shown here:

$$r = \frac{\sum(x_i - \bar{x})(y_i - \bar{y})}{\sqrt{\sum(x_i - \bar{x})^2 \sum(y_i - \bar{y})^2}}$$

Code

You can compute it easily in Python using the following code:

Code block 3-7

```
values_x = [10,8,12,11,7,10,8,9,12,11,10]
values_y = [12,9,11,11,8,11,9,10,14,10,9]

import numpy as np
np.corrcoef(values_x,values_y)
```

You should obtain a correlation matrix in which you can read that the correlation coefficient is 0.77. This indicates a positive correlation between the two variables.

Now that you have seen some numerical ways to describe data, it will be useful to discover some methods for visualizing this data in a more user-friendly way. The following section goes deeper into this.

Real-time visualizations

In this part, you will see how to set up a simple real-time visualization using Plotly's Dash. This tool is a great dashboarding tool for data scientists, as it is easy to learn and does not require much except for a Python environment.

The code is a little bit too long to show in the book, but you can find the Python file (called ch3-realtimeviz.py) in the GitHub repository.

In the code, you can see how a simple real-time graph is built. The general setup of the code is to have an app. You define the layout in the app using HTML-like building blocks. In this case, the layout contains one div (one block of content) in which there is a graph.

The main component is the use of the Interval function in this layout. Using this will make the dashboard update automatically at a given frequency. It is fast enough to consider these as real-time updates.

The callback decorates the function that is written just below it (update_graph). By decorating it this way, the app knows that it has to call this function every time an update is done (triggered by Interval in the layout). The update_graph function returns an updated graph.

Opening the dashboard

Once you run the code on your local machine, you will see the following information:

```
Dash is running on http://127.0.0.1:8050/

 * Serving Flask app "__main__" (lazy loading)
 * Environment: production
   WARNING: This is a development server. Do not use it in a production deployment.
   Use a production WSGI server instead.
 * Debug mode: off

 * Running on http://127.0.0.1:8050/ (Press CTRL+C to quit)
```

Figure 3.1 – Output of Dash

This link will give you access to the dashboard that is being updated in real time. It looks something like this:

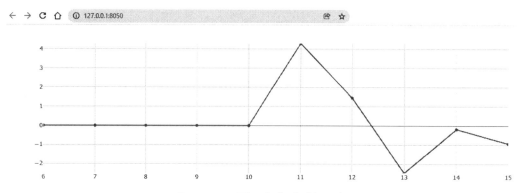

Figure 3.2 – The Plotly dashboard

Comparing Plotly's Dash and other real-time visualization tools

There are many other data visualization tools out there. Popular examples are Power BI, QlikView, and Tableau. The great thing about Plotly's Dash is that it is super easy to get started with if you are already in a Python environment. It is free and does not require installation.

If you want to be a pro in **business intelligence (BI)**, it is worth checking out other tools. Many of them have capacities for real-time updates, and the specific documentation of each tool will guide you to it.

When building dashboarding or data visualization systems, it is also important to consider your overall architecture. As discussed in the previous chapter, in many cases, you will have a data-generating system and an architecture that is able to manage this in real time. Just like any other analytics building block, you will need to make sure that your dashboard can be plugged into your data generating process, or you may need to build an in-between data store or data communication layer.

We will now move on to the next use case of descriptive statistics: building basic alerting systems.

Building basic alerting systems

In the previous parts of this chapter, you have seen an introduction to descriptive statistics and visualization.

Basic alerting systems will be covered as the last data analysis use case. In this part, you will see how you can use basic alerting systems on streaming data. For this, you will see how you can leverage descriptive statistics together with business rules to automatically generate alerts in real time. Example methods for alerting systems are as follows:

- Alerting systems on extreme values
- Alerting systems on process stability
- Alerting systems on constant variability
- Statistical process control and Lean Six Sigma control charts

Alerting systems on extreme values

The first example for alerting and monitoring systems on streaming data is the use case that you have seen in earlier chapters: coding a business rule that sends an alert once observed values are outside of hardcoded boundaries.

This example was coded in previous chapters as follows:

Code block 3-9

```
import pandas as pd
data_batch = pd.DataFrame({
    'tempera-
ture': [10, 11, 10, 11, 12, 11, 10, 9, 10, 11, 12, 11, 9, 12,
11],
    'pH': [5, 5.5, 6, 5, 4.5, 5, 4.5, 5, 4.5, 5, 4, 4.5, 5, 4.
5, 6]
})

data_batch
```

You will see the following data being printed:

	temperature	pH
0	10	5.0
1	11	5.5
2	10	6.0
3	11	5.0
4	12	4.5
5	11	5.0
6	10	4.5
7	9	5.0
8	10	4.5
9	11	5.0
10	12	4.0
11	11	4.5
12	9	5.0
13	12	4.5
14	11	6.0

Figure 3.3 – The data batch

Let's now write the function and loop through the data to execute the function on each data point:

Code block 3-10

```
def super_simple_alert(datapoint):
  if datapoint['temperature'] < 10:
    print('this is a real time alert. Temp too low')
  if datapoint['pH'] > 5.5:
    print('this is a real time alert. pH too high')


data_iterable = data_batch.iterrows()


for i,new_datapoint in data_iterable:
  print(new_datapoint.to_json())
  super_simple_alert(new_datapoint)
```

The resulting print output shows that a number of alerts have been launched:

```
{"temperature":10.0,"pH":5.0}
{"temperature":11.0,"pH":5.5}
{"temperature":10.0,"pH":6.0}
this is a real time alert. pH too high
{"temperature":11.0,"pH":5.0}
{"temperature":12.0,"pH":4.5}
{"temperature":11.0,"pH":5.0}
{"temperature":10.0,"pH":4.5}
{"temperature":9.0,"pH":5.0}
this is a real time alert. temp too low
{"temperature":10.0,"pH":4.5}
{"temperature":11.0,"pH":5.0}
{"temperature":12.0,"pH":4.0}
{"temperature":11.0,"pH":4.5}
{"temperature":9.0,"pH":5.0}
this is a real time alert. temp too low
{"temperature":12.0,"pH":4.5}
{"temperature":11.0,"pH":6.0}
this is a real time alert. pH too high
```

Figure 3.4 – The printed results of your alerting system

This example is a great first step into alerting and monitoring systems: a common use case for streaming data. Let's see how you can build on this example to add more and more complex static logic to this.

Alerting systems on process stability (mean and median)

Rather than applying business logic to individual values, it may be better in some cases to add logic for averages. In many cases, it will not be necessary to send alerts if just one observation is out of specification. However, when the average of several products gets out of specification, you are likely to have a structural problem that needs to be solved.

You could think of coding such an example as follows:

Code block 3-11

```python
import numpy as np
def super_simple_alert(hist_datapoints):
    print(hist_datapoints)
    if np.mean(hist_datapoints['temperature']) < 10:
        print('this is a real time alert. temp too low')
```

```
    if np.mean(hist_datapoints['pH']) > 5.5:
        print('this is a real time alert. pH too high')


data_iterable = data_batch.iterrows()


# create historization for window
hist_temp = []
hist_ph = []


for i,new_datapoint in data_iterable:

    hist_temp.append([new_datapoint['temperature']])
    hist_ph.append([new_datapoint['pH']])

    hist_datapoint = {
        'temperature': hist_temp[-3:],
        'pH': hist_ph[-3:]
    }


    super_simple_alert(hist_datapoint)
```

In this example, you see that there is a windowed average computed on the last 10 observations. This allows you to alert as soon as the average of the last three observations reaches a hardcoded alerting threshold. You should observe the following output:

```
{'temperature': [[10.0]], 'pH': [[5.0]]}
{'temperature': [[10.0], [11.0]], 'pH': [[5.0], [5.5]]}
{'temperature': [[10.0], [11.0], [10.0]], 'pH': [[5.0], [5.5], [6.0]]}
{'temperature': [[11.0], [10.0], [11.0]], 'pH': [[5.5], [6.0], [5.0]]}
{'temperature': [[10.0], [11.0], [12.0]], 'pH': [[6.0], [5.0], [4.5]]}
{'temperature': [[11.0], [12.0], [11.0]], 'pH': [[5.0], [4.5], [5.0]]}
{'temperature': [[12.0], [11.0], [10.0]], 'pH': [[4.5], [5.0], [4.5]]}
{'temperature': [[11.0], [10.0], [9.0]], 'pH': [[5.0], [4.5], [5.0]]}
{'temperature': [[10.0], [9.0], [10.0]], 'pH': [[4.5], [5.0], [4.5]]}
this is a real time alert. temp too low
{'temperature': [[9.0], [10.0], [11.0]], 'pH': [[5.0], [4.5], [5.0]]}
{'temperature': [[10.0], [11.0], [12.0]], 'pH': [[4.5], [5.0], [4.0]]}
{'temperature': [[11.0], [12.0], [11.0]], 'pH': [[5.0], [4.0], [4.5]]}
{'temperature': [[12.0], [11.0], [9.0]], 'pH': [[4.0], [4.5], [5.0]]}
{'temperature': [[11.0], [9.0], [12.0]], 'pH': [[4.5], [5.0], [4.5]]}
{'temperature': [[9.0], [12.0], [11.0]], 'pH': [[5.0], [4.5], [6.0]]}
```

Figure 3.5 – Improved print output

You can observe that the fact of using the average of three observations makes it much less likely to receive an alert. If you were to use even more observations in your window, this would be reduced even more. Fine-tuning should depend on the business case.

Alerting systems on constant variability (std and variance)

You can do the same with variability. As discussed in the section on descriptive statistics, a process is often described by centrality and variability. Even if your average is within specifications, there may be a large variability; if variability is large, this may be a problem for you as well.

You can do alerting systems on variability using windowed computations of the mean. This can be used for a dashboard, but also for alerting systems and more.

You can code this as follows:

Code block 3-12

```python
import numpy as np
def super_simple_alert(hist_datapoints):
  print(hist_datapoints)
  if np.std(hist_datapoints['temperature']) > 1:
    print('this is a real time alert. temp varia-
tions too high')
  if np.std(hist_datapoints['pH']) > 1:
    print('this is a real time alert. pH variations too high')
data_iterable = data_batch.iterrows()
# create historization for window
hist_temp = []
hist_ph = []
for i,new_datapoint in data_iterable:
  hist_temp.append([new_datapoint['temperature']])
  hist_ph.append([new_datapoint['pH']])
  hist_datapoint = {
      'temperature': hist_temp[-3:],
      'pH': hist_ph[-3:]
  }
  super_simple_alert(hist_datapoint)
```

Note that the alerts are now not based on the average value, but on variability. You will receive the following output for this example:

```
{'temperature': [[10.0]], 'pH': [[5.0]]}
{'temperature': [[10.0], [11.0]], 'pH': [[5.0], [5.5]]}
{'temperature': [[10.0], [11.0], [10.0]], 'pH': [[5.0], [5.5], [6.0]]}
{'temperature': [[11.0], [10.0], [11.0]], 'pH': [[5.5], [6.0], [5.0]]}
{'temperature': [[10.0], [11.0], [12.0]], 'pH': [[6.0], [5.0], [4.5]]}
{'temperature': [[11.0], [12.0], [11.0]], 'pH': [[5.0], [4.5], [5.0]]}
{'temperature': [[12.0], [11.0], [10.0]], 'pH': [[4.5], [5.0], [4.5]]}
{'temperature': [[11.0], [10.0], [9.0]], 'pH': [[5.0], [4.5], [5.0]]}
{'temperature': [[10.0], [9.0], [10.0]], 'pH': [[4.5], [5.0], [4.5]]}
{'temperature': [[9.0], [10.0], [11.0]], 'pH': [[5.0], [4.5], [5.0]]}
{'temperature': [[10.0], [11.0], [12.0]], 'pH': [[4.5], [5.0], [4.0]]}
{'temperature': [[11.0], [12.0], [11.0]], 'pH': [[5.0], [4.0], [4.5]]}
{'temperature': [[12.0], [11.0], [9.0]], 'pH': [[4.0], [4.5], [5.0]]}
this is a real time alert. temp variations too high
{'temperature': [[11.0], [9.0], [12.0]], 'pH': [[4.5], [5.0], [4.5]]}
this is a real time alert. temp variations too high
{'temperature': [[9.0], [12.0], [11.0]], 'pH': [[5.0], [4.5], [6.0]]}
this is a real time alert. temp variations too high
```

Figure 3.6 – Even further improved print output

Basic alerting systems using statistical process control

If you want to go a step further with this type of alert system, you can use methods from statistical process control. This domain of statistics focuses on controlling a process or a production method. The main tool that stems from this domain is called **control charts**.

In control charts, you plot a statistic over time, but you add control limits. A standard control chart is the one in which you plot the sample average over time, and you add control limits based on standard deviation. You then count and observe a number of extreme values and when a certain number of repetitive events occur, you launch an alert.

You will find a link in the *Further reading* section for more details on control charts and statistical process control.

Summary

In this chapter, you have learned the basics of doing data analysis on streaming data. You have seen that doing descriptive statistics on data streams does not work the same as when doing descriptive statistics on batch data. Estimation theory from batch data can be used, but you have to window over data to get a larger or smaller window of historical data.

Windowing settings can have a strong impact on your results. Larger windows will take into account more data and will be taking into account data further back in time. They will, however, be much less sensitive to the new data point. After all, the larger the window, the lesser impact one new data point has.

You have also learned how to build data visualizations using Plotly's Dash. This tool is great, as it is quite powerful and can still be used from a Python environment. Many other visualization tools exist, but the most important thing is to master at least one of them. This chapter has shown you the functional requirements for visualizing streaming data, and you'll be able to reproduce this on other data visualization tools if needed.

The last part of the chapter introduced statistical process control. Until now, you have been working with static rules or descriptive statistics for building simple alerting systems. Statistical process control is an interesting domain for building more advanced alerting systems that are still relatively easy to comprehend and implement.

In the next chapter, you will start discovering online machine learning. Once you get familiarized with online machine learning in general, you'll see, in later chapters, how you can replace static decision rules for alerting systems with machine learning-based anomaly detection models. The data analysis methods that you have seen in this chapter are an important first step in that direction.

Further reading

- *Estimation theory*: https://en.wikipedia.org/wiki/Estimation_theory
- *Sampling*: https://en.wikipedia.org/wiki/Sampling_(statistics)
- *Windowing*: https://softwaremill.com/windowing-in-big-data-streams-spark-flink-kafka-akka/
- *Plot live graphs using Python Dash and Plotly*: https://www.geeksforgeeks.org/plot-live-graphs-using-python-dash-and-plotly/
- Plotly Dash documentation: https://plotly.com/
- Control charts: https://en.wikipedia.org/wiki/Control_chart
- *Engineering Statistics Handbook, Chapter 6.3 Univariate and Multivariate Control Charts*: https://www.itl.nist.gov/div898/handbook/pmc/section3/pmc3.htm

Part 2: Exploring Use Cases for Data Streaming

This section covers different machine learning techniques for streaming data, including a lot of online models as well as reinforcement learning.

This section comprises the following chapters:

4

Online Learning with River

In this and the coming three chapters, you will learn how to work with a library for online machine learning called River. Online machine learning is a part of machine learning in which models are designed in such a way that they can update their learned model on the reception of any new data point.

Online machine learning is the opposite of offline machine learning, which is the regular machine learning that you are probably already aware of. In general, in machine learning, a model will try to learn a mathematical rule that can perform a certain task. This task is learned on the basis of a number of data points. The mathematics behind these tasks is based on statistics and algorithmics.

In this chapter, you will discover how to work with online machine learning, and you will discover multiple types of online machine learning. You will go more in depth into the differences between online and offline machine learning. You will also see how to build online machine learning models using River in Python.

This chapter covers the following topics:

- What is online machine learning?
- River for online learning
- A super simple example with River
- A second example with River

Technical requirements

You can find all the code for this book on GitHub at the following link: `https://github.com/PacktPublishing/Machine-Learning-for-Streaming-Data-with-Python`. If you are not yet familiar with Git and GitHub, the easiest way to download the notebooks and code samples is the following:

1. Go to the link of the repository.
2. Go to the green **Code** button.
3. Select **Download ZIP**.

When you download the ZIP file, unzip it in your local environment, and you will be able to access the code through your preferred Python editor.

Python environment

To follow along with this book, you can download the code in the repository and execute it using your preferred Python editor.

If you are not yet familiar with Python environments, I would advise you to check out Anaconda (`https://www.anaconda.com/products/individual`), which comes with the Jupyter Notebook and JupyterLabs, which are both great for executing notebooks. It also comes with Spyder and VSCode for editing scripts and programs.

If you have difficulty installing Python or the associated programs on your machine, you can check out Google Colab (`https://colab.research.google.com/`) or Kaggle Notebooks (`https://www.kaggle.com/code`), which both allow you to run Python code in online notebooks for free, without any setup to do.

> **Note**
> The code in the book will generally use Colab and Kaggle notebooks with Python version 3.7.13 and you can set up your own environment to mimic this.

What is online machine learning?

In machine learning, the most common way to train a model is to do a single training pass. The general steps in this approach are as follows:

1. Data preparation.
2. Create a train-test split.
3. Do model benchmarking and hyperparameter tuning.
4. Select the best model.
5. Move this model to production.

This approach is called **offline learning**.

With streaming data, you can often use this type of model very well. You can build the model once, deploy it, and use it for predicting your input stream. You can probably track the performance metrics of your model, and when the performance starts to change, you can do an update or retraining of your model, deploy the new version, and let it set in the production environment as long as it works.

Online machine learning is a branch of machine learning that contains models that work very differently. They do not learn a full dataset at once, but rather, update the learned model (the decision rules for prediction) through sequential steps. Using such an approach, you can automatically update your model that is in production; it continues to learn on new data.

How is online learning different from regular learning?

The practice of building online learning systems takes a different angle at the machine learning problem than the offline machine learning approach. With offline learning, there is a real possibility to test what a model has learned, whereas, for online learning systems, this can change at any moment.

For some use cases, it is impossible to use offline learning. An example is forecasting use cases. In general, for forecasting, you predict a value in the future. To do so, you use the most recent data available to train and retrain your model. In many forecasting applications, machine learning models are retrained every time a new forecast must be predicted.

Outlier detection is another example where offline learning can be less appropriate. If your model does not integrate each new data point, these data points cannot be used as reference cases against new values. This can be solved through offline learning as well, but online learning may be the more appropriate solution to tackle this use case.

Advantages of online learning

Online learning has two main advantages:

- The first main advantage is that online learning algorithms can be updated. They can, therefore, learn in multiple passes. This way, a big dataset does not have to pass at once in a model but can be passed in multiple steps. This is a big advantage when the datasets are large, or when the computing resources are limited.

- The second advantage of online learning is that an online model can adapt to newer processes when updating: it is less fixed. Therefore, where an offline model can become obsolete when data trends change slightly over time, an online model can adapt to these changes and remain performant.

Challenges of online learning

However, there are also disadvantages to using online learning.

First, the concept is less widespread, and it will be a bit harder to find model implementations and documentation for online learning use cases.

Second, and more important, online learning has a risk of models learning things that you don't want them to learn or things that are wrong. With offline learning, you have much more control to validate what a model learns before pushing it to a production environment, whereas when pushing online learning to production environments, it may well continue to learn and decrease in performance due to the updates that it has learned.

Now that you understand the concept of online learning, let's now discover multiple types of online learning.

Types of online learning

Although there is no clearly defined distinction in types of online machine learning, it is good to consider at least the following three terms: incremental learning, adaptive learning, and reinforcement learning.

Incremental learning

Incremental learning methods are models that can be updated with a single observation at a time. As described previously, one of the main added values of online machine learning is this, as this is something that is not possible with standard offline learning.

Adaptive learning

Just updating the model, however, may not be enough for the second important added value of online learning that was cited before. If you want a model to adapt well to more recent data, you will have to choose an **adaptive** online learning method. These methods deal well with any situation that would need a model to adapt, for example, new trends that appear in the underlying data before people even become aware of them.

Reinforcement learning

Reinforcement learning is not necessarily considered a subfield of online learning. Although the approach of reinforcement learning is different than the previously cited online learning approaches, it can be used for the same business problems. It is, therefore, important to learn about reinforcement learning as well. It will be covered in more depth in a later chapter. In the coming section, you will see how to use the River package in Python to build online machine learning models.

Using River for online learning

In this section, you will discover the River library for online learning. River is a Python library that is made specifically for online machine learning. Its code base is a result of the combination of the `creme` and the `scikit-multiflow` libraries. The goal of River is to become the go-to library for machine learning on streaming data.

In this example, you'll see how to train an online model on a well-known dataset. The steps that you will take throughout this example are the following:

1. Import the data.
2. Reclassify the data to obtain a binary classification problem.
3. Fit an online model for binary classification.
4. Improve the model evaluation using a train-test split.
5. Fit an online multiclass classification model using one-vs-rest.

Training an online model with River

For this example, you will use the well-known iris dataset. You can download it from the UCI machine learning repository, but you can also use the following code to download it directly into pandas.

The steps to get to our goal are as follows:

1. Importing the data
2. Reclassifying the data into a binary problem
3. Converting the data into a suitable input format
4. Learning the model one data point at a time
5. Evaluating the model

We will get started using the following steps:

1. We will first import the dataset as seen here:

Code Block 4-1

```
#iris dataset classification example
import pandas as pd
colnames = ['sepal_length','sepal_width','petal_
length','petal_width','class']
data = pd.read_csv('https://archive.ics.uci.
edu/ml/machine-learning-databases/iris/iris.
data', names=colnames)
data.head()
```

The dataset looks as follows:

	sepal_length	sepal_width	petal_length	petal_width	class
0	5.1	3.5	1.4	0.2	Iris-setosa
1	4.9	3.0	1.4	0.2	Iris-setosa
2	4.7	3.2	1.3	0.2	Iris-setosa
3	4.6	3.1	1.5	0.2	Iris-setosa
4	5.0	3.6	1.4	0.2	Iris-setosa
...	...	...	...	...	...
145	6.7	3.0	5.2	2.3	Iris-virginica
146	6.3	2.5	5.0	1.9	Iris-virginica
147	6.5	3.0	5.2	2.0	Iris-virginica
148	6.2	3.4	5.4	2.3	Iris-virginica
149	5.9	3.0	5.1	1.8	Iris-virginica

150 rows × 5 columns

Figure 4.1 – The iris dataset

The iris dataset is very commonly used, mainly in tutorials and examples. The dataset contains a number of observations of three different iris species, a type of flower. For each flower, you have the length and width of specific parts of the plant. You can use the four variables to predict the species of iris.

2. For this first model, you will need to convert the class column into a binary column, as you will use the `LogisticRegression` model from River, which does not support multiclass:

Code Block 4-2

```
data['setosa'] = data['class'] == 'Iris-setosa'
data['setosa']
```

This results in the following output:

```
Out[76]: 0       True
         1       True
         2       True
         3       True
         4       True
                 ...
         145     False
         146     False
         147     False
         148     False
         149     False
Name: setosa, Length: 150, dtype: bool
```

Figure 4.2 – The series with Boolean data type

3. As a next step, we will write code to loop through the data to simulate a streaming data input. The X data should be in dictionary format, and y can be string, int, or Boolean. In the following code, you see a loop that stops after the first iteration, so that it prints one X and one y:

Code Block 4-3

```
# convert to streaming dataset
for i, row in data.sample(1).iterrows():
    X = row[['sepal_length', 'sepal_width', 'petal_
length', 'petal_width']]
    X = X.to_dict()


    y = row['setosa']
```

```
print (X)
print (y)
break
```

You can see that X has to be in a dictionary format, which is relatively uncommon for those who are familiar with offline learning. Then, y can be either Boolean, a string, or an int. This will look as follows:

```
{"sepal_length":6.1,"sepal_width":3.0,"petal_length":4.6,"petal_width":1.4}
False
```

Figure 4.3 – The x and y inputs for the model

4. Now, let's fit the model one by one. It is important to add .sample(frac=1) to avoid getting the data in order. If you do not add this, the model would first receive all the data from one class and then from the other classes. The model has a hard time dealing with that, so a random order should be introduced using the sample function:

Code Block 4-4

```
!pip install river
from river import linear_model


model =  linear_model.LogisticRegression()
for i,row in data.sample(frac=1).iterrows():
    X = row[['sepal_length', 'sepal_width', 'petal_
length', 'petal_width']]
    X = X.to_dict()
    y = row['setosa']


    model.learn_one(X, y)
```

5. Let's see how the predictions can be made on the training data. You can use predict_many to predict on a data frame, or else you can use predict_one:

Code Block 4-5

```
preds = model.predict_many(data[['sepal_length', 'sepal_
width', 'petal_length', 'petal_width']])
print(preds)
```

The result looks as follows:

```
Out[68]:  0      True
          1      True
          2      True
          3      True
          4      True
                 ...
          145    False
          146    False
          147    False
          148    False
          149    False
          Length: 150, dtype: bool
```

Figure 4.4 – The 150 Boolean observations

6. You can use the `scikit-learn` accuracy score to estimate the training accuracy of this model:

Code Block 4-6

```
from sklearn.metrics import accuracy_score
accuracy_score(data['setosa'], preds)
```

The obtained training accuracy, in this case, is 1, indicating that the model has perfectly learned the training data. Although the model has learned perfect prediction on the data that it has seen during the learning process, it is unlikely that the performance would be as good on new, unseen data points. In the next section, we will improve our model evaluation so that we avoid having overestimated performance metrics.

Improving the model evaluation

In the first example, there was no real relearning and updating.

In this example, we will update and track the accuracy throughout the learning process. You will also see how to keep a training and separate test set. You can use each data point for learning once it arrives, and you will use the updated model for the prediction of the next data point to arrive. This more closely resembles a streaming use case.

The steps to get there are as follows:

1. Train-test split.

2. Fit the model on the training data.

3. Check out the learning curve.

4. Compute performance metrics on the test data.

We will get started as follows:

1. Let's start with a stratified train-test split on the data:

Code Block 4-7

```
# add a stratified train test split
from sklearn.model_selection import train_test_split
train,test = train_test_
split(data, stratify =data['setosa'])
```

2. You can now redo the same learning loop as before but on the training data. You can see that there is a list called correct to track how the learning has gone over time:

Code Block 4-8

```
from river import linear_model,metrics


model =  linear_model.LogisticRegression()
correct = []


for i,row in train.sample(frac=1).iterrows():
    X = row[['sepal_length', 'sepal_width', 'petal_
length', 'petal_width']]
    X = X.to_dict()


    y = row['setosa']


    model.predict_one(X)
    correct.append(y == model.predict_one(X))


    model.learn_one(X,y)
```

3. Let's plot the cumulative sum of `correct` scores over time, to see whether the model learned well from the beginning, or whether the model had fewer errors at the end of the learning curve:

Code Block 4-9

```
# this model is learning quite stable from the start

import matplotlib.pyplot as plt
import numpy as np

plt.plot(np.cumsum(correct))
```

You can see that the learning curve is quite linear; the accuracy stays more or less constant over time. It would have been expected to see an improvement in accuracy over time (more correct responses over time, with an exponential-like curve) if the ml was actually improving with training. You can check out the learning curve in the following graph:

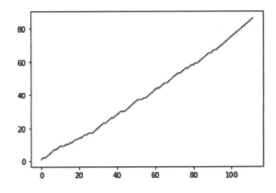

Figure 4.5 – The learning curve

4. Finally, let's compute the accuracy on the test score to see how well the model generates out-of-sample data:

Code Block 4-10

```
# model was not so good on out of sample
accuracy_score(test['setosa'],model.predict_
many(test[['sepal_length', 'sepal_width', 'petal_
length', 'petal_width']]))
```

The score that this obtained is 0.94, which is slightly lower than the 1.0 obtained on the train set. This teaches us that the model learned quite well.

In the coming chapters, you'll see more tricks and tools that can help improve models and accuracy.

Building a multiclass classifier using one-vs-rest

In the previous example, you have seen how to build a binary classifier. To do this, you reclassified the target variable into *setosa-vs-rest*. However, you would want to build one model that allows you to do all of the three classes at the same time. This can be done using River's OneVsRest classifier. Let's now see an example of this:

1. You can start with the same train-test split as before, except that now, you can stratify on the class:

Code Block 4-11

```
# add a stratified train test split
from sklearn.model_selection import train_test_split
train,test = train_test_
split(data, stratify =data['class'])
```

2. You then fit the model on the training data. The code is almost the same, except that you use OneVsRestClassifier around the call to LogisticRegression:

Code Block 4-12

```
from river import linear_model,metrics,multiclass
model =   multiclass.OneVsRestClassifier(linear_model.
LogisticRegression())
correct = []


for i,row in train.sample(frac=1).iterrows():
    X = row[['sepal_length', 'sepal_width', 'petal_
length', 'petal_width']]
    X = X.to_dict()


    y = row['class']


    model.predict_one(X)
```

```
correct.append(y == model.predict_one(X))

model.learn_one(X,y)
```

3. When looking at the learning over time, you can see that the model has started learning better after around 40 observations. Before 40 observations, it had much fewer correct predictions than after:

Code Block 4-13

```
# this model predicts better after 40 observations

import matplotlib.pyplot as plt
import numpy as np

plt.plot(np.cumsum(correct))
```

The plot looks as follows. It clearly has a less steep slope in the first 40 observations and accuracy improves after that:

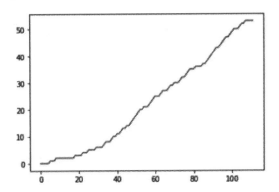

Figure 4.6 – A better learning curve

4. You can again use predict_many to see whether the predictions are any good. When doing predict, you will now not have True/False, but instead, have the string values of each of the iris types:

Code Block 4-14

```
model.predict_many(test[['sepal_length', 'sepal_
width', 'petal_length', 'petal_width']])
```

This results in the following output:

```
132    Iris-versicolor
95     Iris-versicolor
111    Iris-versicolor
89     Iris-versicolor
25         Iris-setosa
105    Iris-versicolor
139    Iris-versicolor
33         Iris-setosa
62     Iris-versicolor
66     Iris-versicolor
45         Iris-setosa
63     Iris-versicolor
32         Iris-setosa
29         Iris-setosa
86     Iris-versicolor
57     Iris-versicolor
dtype: object
```

Figure 4.7 – The multiclass target

5. The test accuracy of the model can be computed using the following code:

Code Block 4-15

```
# model scores 0.63 on the test data
from sklearn.metrics import accuracy_score
accuracy_score(test['class'],model.predict_
many(test[['sepal_length', 'sepal_width', 'petal_
length', 'petal_width']]))
```

The model obtains an accuracy score of 0.63 on the test data.

Summary

In this chapter, you have learned the basics of online machine learning in both theory and practice. You have seen different types of online machine learning, including incremental, adaptive, and reinforcement learning.

You have seen a number of advantages and disadvantages of online machine learning. Among other reasons, you may be almost obliged to refer to online methods if quick relearning is required. A disadvantage is that fewer methods are commonly available, as batch learning remains the industry standard for now.

Finally, you have started practicing and implementing online machine learning through a Python example on the well-known iris dataset.

In the coming chapter, you'll go much deeper into online machine learning, focusing on anomaly detection. You'll see how machine learning can be used to replace the fixed rule alerting system that was built in previous chapters. In the chapters after that, you'll learn more about online classification and regression using River with examples that continue the learnings from the iris classification model from the current chapter.

Further reading

- *UCI Machine Learning Repository*: https://archive.ics.uci.edu/ml/index.php

- River ML: https://riverml.xyz/latest/

- *Online Machine Learning*: https://en.wikipedia.org/wiki/Online_machine_learning

- *Incremental Learning*: https://en.wikipedia.org/wiki/Incremental_learning

- *Reinforcement Learning*: https://en.wikipedia.org/wiki/Reinforcement_learning

- Logistic Regression: https://www.statisticssolutions.com/free-resources/directory-of-statistical-analyses/what-is-logistic-regression/

- One vs Rest: https://stats.stackexchange.com/questions/167623/understanding-the-one-vs-the-rest-classifier

- *Multiclass classification*: https://en.wikipedia.org/wiki/Multiclass_classification

- scikit-learn metrics: https://scikit-learn.org/stable/modules/model_evaluation.html

5

Online Anomaly Detection

Anomaly detection is a good starting point for machine learning on streaming data. As streaming data delivers a continuous stream of data points, use cases of monitoring live solutions are among the first that come to mind.

There are many domains in which monitoring is essential. In IT solutions, there is generally continuous logging of what happens in the systems, and those logs can be analyzed as streaming data.

In the **Internet of Things (IoT)**, sensor data is being collected on sometimes a large number of sensors. This data is then analyzed and used in real time.

Real-time and online anomaly detection can be of great added value in such use cases by finding values that are far from the expected range of measurements, or otherwise unexpected. Detecting them on time can have great value.

In this chapter, you will first get an in-depth overview of anomaly detection and the theoretical considerations to take into account when implementing it. You will then see how to implement online anomaly detection using the River package in Python.

This chapter covers the following topics:

- Defining anomaly detection
- Use cases of anomaly detection
- Comparing anomaly detection and imbalanced classification
- Algorithms for detecting anomalies in River
- Going further with anomaly detection

Technical requirements

You can find all the code for this book on GitHub at the following link: `https://github.com/PacktPublishing/Machine-Learning-for-Streaming-Data-with-Python`. If you are not yet familiar with Git and GitHub, the easiest way to download the notebooks and code samples is the following:

1. Go to the link of the repository.
2. Go to the green **Code** button.
3. Select **Download ZIP**.

When you download the ZIP file, unzip it in your local environment, and you will be able to access the code through your preferred Python editor.

Python environment

To follow along with this book, you can download the code in the repository and execute it using your preferred Python editor.

If you are not yet familiar with Python environments, I would advise you to check out Anaconda (`https://www.anaconda.com/products/individual`), which comes with Jupyter Notebooks and JupyterLabs, which are both great for executing notebooks. It also comes with Spyder and VSCode for editing scripts and programs.

If you have difficulty installing Python or the associated programs on your machine, you can check out Google Colab (`https://colab.research.google.com/`) or Kaggle Notebooks (`https://www.kaggle.com/code`), which both allow you to run Python code in online notebooks for free, without any setup to do.

Defining anomaly detection

Let's start by creating an understanding of what **anomaly detection** is. Also called outlier detection, anomaly detection is the process of identifying rare observations in a dataset. Those rare observations are called **outliers** or **anomalies**.

The goal of anomaly detection is to build models that can automatically detect outliers using statistical methods and/or machine learning. Such models can use multiple variables to see whether an observation should be considered an outlier or not.

Are outliers a problem?

Outliers occur in many datasets. After all, if you consider a variable that follows a normal distribution, it is normal to see data points far away from the mean. Let's consider a standard normal distribution (a normal distribution with mean 0 and standard deviation 1):

Code Block 5-1

```
import matplotlib.pyplot as plt
import numpy as np
import scipy.stats as stats


x = np.linspace(-4,4, 100)
plt.plot(x, stats.norm.pdf(x, 0, 1))
```

You can see the resulting figure as follows:

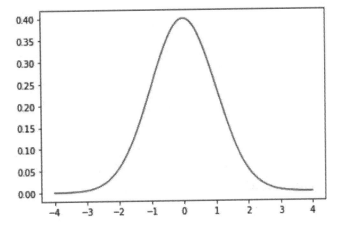

Figure 5.1 – The normal distribution

This standard normal distribution has most of its observations around 0. However, it is normal to observe some observations in the tails of the distribution. If you have a variable that really follows this distribution, and your sample size is big enough, having some observations far away from the center cannot really be considered something bad.

In the following code, you see how a sample of 10 million observations is drawn from a standard normal distribution:

Code Block 5-2

```
import numpy as np
import matplotlib.pyplot as plt
data = np.random.normal(size=10000000)
plt.hist(data, bins=25)
```

The data follows the normal curve quite well. You can see this in the following graph:

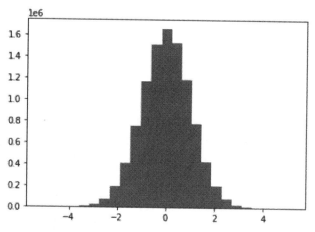

Figure 5.2 – The normal distribution histogram

Now, let's see what the highest and lowest values of this sample are by using the following code:

Code Block 5-3

```
min(data), max(data)
```

In the current draw, a minimum of 5.11 and a maximum of 5.12 were observed. Now, are those outliers or not? The answer is complicated. Of course, the two values are perfectly within the range of the normal distribution. On the other hand, they are extreme values.

This example illustrates that defining an outlier is not always easy, and needs careful consideration for your specific use case. We will now see a number of use cases of anomaly detection.

Exploring use cases of anomaly detection

Before moving on to some specific algorithms for anomaly detection, let's first consider some use cases that are often done with anomaly detection.

Fraud detection in financial institutions

A very common use case for anomaly detection is the detection of fraud in financial institutions. Banks generally have a lot of data, as almost everyone has one or more bank accounts that are used on a regular basis. All these usages generate a huge amount of data that can help banks to improve their services and their profits. Fraud detection is a key component of data science applications in banks, together with many other use cases.

A common use case for fraud detection is to automatically detect credit card fraud. Imagine that your card or card details have been stolen and someone is fraudulently using them. This leads to fraudulent transactions, which could be automatically detected by a machine learning algorithm. The bank could then automatically block your card and ask you to validate whether it was you, or someone fraudulently making these payments.

This is both in the interest of the bank and of the user, so it is a great use case for anomaly detection. Other companies that work with credit card and payment data may also use these methods.

Streaming models are great for fraud detection. There is generally a huge amount of data that comes in in a continuous stream of payments and other data. Streaming models allow you to take action directly when a fraud situation occurs, rather than waiting for the next batch to be launched.

If you want to read more about fraud detection in financial institutions, you can check out the following links:

- `https://www.miteksystems.com/blog/how-does-machine-learning-help-with-fraud-detection-in-banks`
- `https://www.sas.com/en_us/software/detection-investigation-for-banking.html`

Anomaly detection on your log data

A second use case for anomaly detection is log analysis. Many software applications generate huge amounts of logs containing all types of information on the execution of programs. These logs are often stored temporarily or long-term for further analysis. In some cases, these analyses may be manual searches of specific information about what happened at some point in software, but at other times they may be automated log treatment programs.

One of the difficulties with anomaly detection in logs is that log data is generally very unstructured. Often, they are just a bunch of printed statements one after the other in a text file. It is very hard to make sense of this data.

If you succeed in the challenge of structuring and categorizing your log data correctly, you can then use machine learning techniques to automatically detect problems with the execution of your software. This allows you to take action straight away.

Using streaming analysis rather than batch analysis is important here as well. Some software is mission-critical, and downtime often means problems for the company. These can be different types of problems, including contractual problems and loss of revenue. If a company can automatically detect bugs, this allows them to move fast and quickly repair the problems. The faster a problem is repaired, the fewer problems for the company.

For deeper use case literature on anomaly detection on log data, you can have a look at the following links:

- `https://www.zebrium.com/blog/using-machine-learning-to-detect-anomalies-in-logs`
- `https://arxiv.org/abs/2202.04301`

Fault detection in manufacturing and production lines

An example of fault detection in production lines is the business of industrial food production. Many production lines are almost fully automated, meaning that there is almost no human intervention between the input of raw products and the output of finalized products. The risk of this is that defects might be occurring that cannot be accepted as final products.

The use of sensor data on production lines can strongly help in detecting anomalies in production. When a production line has some parameters that go wrong, sensors, in combination with streaming systems and real-time alerting systems, can allow you to stop the production of faulty products immediately. This can save a lot of money, as producing waste is very costly.

Using streaming and real-time analytics here is also important. The longer you take to respond to a problem, the more waste you produce and the more money is lost. There is a huge return on investment to gain from implementing real-time and streaming analytics systems in manufacturing and production lines.

The following links will allow you to learn more about this use case:

- `https://www.scienced irect.com/science/article/pii/S2212827119301908`
- `https://www.merl.com/publications/docs/TR2018-097.pdf`

Hacking detection in computer networks (cyber security)

Automated threat detection for cyber security is another great use case of anomaly detection. Just like the other use cases, positive occurrences are very rare compared to negative cases. The importance of those positive cases, however, is far more impactful than the negative ones.

With recent developments, there is a much higher impact of cyber security problems and leaks for companies than before. Personal data can be sold for a large amount of money and hackers often try to steal this information thinking that they can remain anonymous behind their computers.

Threat and anomaly detection systems are automated systems using machine learning to detect behavior that is not normal and that may represent intrusions. If companies can react quickly to such events happening, they can avoid large public shaming campaigns and potential lawsuits costing lots of money.

Streaming and real-time systems are crucial here as well, as leaving as little time as possible for intruders to act will strongly reduce the risk of any cyber criminality happening in your organization.

The following two articles give a good deep dive into such use cases:

- `https://securityboulevard.com/2021/07/what-is-anomaly-detection-in-cybersecurity/`
- `https://www.xenonstack.com/insights/cyber-network-security`

Medical risks in health data

The medical world has seen a large number of inventions over the last years. Part of this is in personal tools such as smart watches and other connected health devices that allow you to measure your own health KPIs in real time. Other use cases can be found in hospitals and other professional health care applications.

When anomalies occur in your health KPIs, it is often of utmost importance to intervene straight away. Health KPI signals can often occur even before we, as humans, start to notice that our health is deteriorating. Even if it is shortly after an event happens, the information will be able to get you the right care without spending much time looking for resources on the causes of your problem.

In general, most of your health metrics will be good, or at least acceptable, until that one metric tells you that something is really going wrong and you need help. In such scenarios, it is important to work with streaming analytics rather than batch analytics. After all, if the data arrives the next hour or the next day, it may well be too late for you. This is another strong argument for using streaming analytics rather than batch analytics.

You can read more about this over here:

- `https://medinform.jmir.org/2021/5/e27172/`
- `https://arxiv.org/pdf/2012.02364.pdf`

Predictive maintenance and sensor data

The last use case that will be discussed here is the use case of predictive maintenance. Many companies have critical systems that need preventive maintenance; if something breaks, this will cost a lot of money or even worse.

An example is the aviation industry. If an airplane crashes, this costs a lot of lives. Of course, no company can predict all anomalies, but any anomaly that could be detected before a crash happens would be a great win.

Anomaly detections can be used for predictive maintenance in many sectors that have comparable problems; if you can predict that your critical system will fail soon, you can have just enough time to do maintenance on the part that needs it and avoid larger problems.

Predictive maintenance can sometimes be done in batch, but it can also benefit from streaming. It all depends on the amount of time you have between detecting an anomaly and the intervention being needed.

If you have a predictive maintenance model that predicts airplane engine failure between now and 30 minutes, you have a large need to get this data to your pilot as soon as possible. If you have predictive systems that tell you that a part needs changing in the coming month, you can probably use batch analytics as well.

To read more about this use case, you can check out the following links:

- `https://www.knime.com/blog/anomaly-detection-for-predictive-maintenance-EDA`

- `https://www.e3s-conferences.org/articles/e3sconf/pdf/2020/30/e3sconf_evf2020_02007.pdf`

In the next section, you will see how anomaly detection models compare to imbalanced classification.

Comparing anomaly detection and imbalanced classification

For detecting positive cases against negative cases, the standard go-to family of methods would be classification. For the problems described, as long as you have historical data on at least a few positive and negative cases, you can use classification algorithms. However, you have a very common problem: there are only very few observations that are anomalies. This is a problem that is generally known as the problem of **imbalanced data**.

The problem of imbalanced data

Imbalanced datasets are datasets in which the target class has very unevenly distributed occurrences. An often-occurring example is website sales: among 1,000 visitors, you often have at least 900 visitors that are just watching and browsing, as opposed to maybe 100 who actually buy something.

Using classification methods carelessly on imbalanced data is prone to errors. Imagine that you fit a classification model that needs to predict for each website visitor whether they will buy something. If you create a very bad model that only predicts non-buying for every visitor, then you will still be right for 900 out of the 1,000 visitors and your accuracy metric will be 90%.

There are a number of standard approaches against this imbalanced data, including using the F1 score and using SMOTE oversampling.

The F1 score

The F1 score is a great replacement for the accuracy score in cases of unbalanced data. Accuracy is computed as the number of correct predictions divided by the total number of predictions made.

This is the formula for accuracy:

$$Accuracy = \frac{\#\ of\ correct\ predictions}{\#\ of\ total\ predictions}$$

The F1 score, however, takes into account the precision and recall of your model. The precision of a model is the percentage of predicted positives that are actually correct. The recall of your model shows the percentage of positives that you were actually able to detect.

This is the formula of precision:

$$Precision = \frac{\#\ of\ True\ Positives}{\#\ of\ True\ Positives + \#\ of\ False\ Positives}$$

This is the formula of recall:

$$Recall = \frac{\#\ of\ True\ Positives}{\#\ of\ True\ Positives + \#\ of\ False\ Negatives}$$

The F1 score combines those two into one metric, using the following formula:

$$F1\ Score = 2 * \frac{Precision * Recall}{Precision + Recall}$$

Using this metric for evaluation, you will avoid interpreting very bad models as good models, especially in the case of imbalanced data.

SMOTE oversampling

SMOTE oversampling is the second method that you can use for counteracting imbalance in your data. It is a method that will create *fake* data points that strongly resemble the data points in your positive class. By creating a number of data points, your model will be able to learn much better about the positive class, and by using the original positives as the source, you guarantee that the newly generated data points are not too far off.

Anomaly detection versus classification

Although imbalanced classification problems can sometimes work well for anomaly detection problems, there is a reason that anomaly detection is treated as a separate category of machine learning.

The main difference is in the importance of understanding what the positive (anomaly) class looks like. In classification models, you want a model that is easily able to distinguish between two (positives and negatives) or more classes. For this to work, you want your model to learn what each class looks like. The model will search for variables that describe one class, and for other variables or values that describe the other class.

In anomaly detection, you don't really care what the anomaly class looks like. What you need much more, is your model to learn what is *normal*. As long as your model has a very good understanding of the normal, negative class, it will be able to state normal versus abnormal quite well. This can be an anomaly in any direction and in any sense of the word. It is not needed for the model to have seen such a type of anomaly before, just to know that it is not normal.

In the case of a first anomaly, a standard classification model would not know what this observation should be classified into. If you're lucky, it could go into the anomaly class, but you have no reason to believe it will. However, an anomaly detection model that focuses on what it knows versus what it does not know would be able to detect this anomaly as something that it has not seen before and, therefore, class it as an anomaly.

In the next section, you will see a number of algorithms for anomaly detection that are available in Python's River package.

Algorithms for detecting anomalies in River

In this chapter, you will again use River for online machine learning algorithms. There are other libraries out there, but River is a very promising candidate for being the go-to Python package for online learning (except for reinforcement learning).

You will see two of the online machine learning algorithms for anomaly detection that River currently (version 0.9.0) contains, as follows:

- `OneClassSVM`: An online adaptation of the offline version of One-Class SVM
- `HalfSpaceTrees`: An online adaptation of Isolation Forests

You will also see how to work with the constant thresholder and the quantile thresholder.

The use of thresholders in River anomaly detection

Let's first look at the use of thresholders, as they will be wrapped around the actual anomaly detection algorithms.

Anomaly detection algorithms will generally return a score between 0 and 1 to indicate to the model to what extent the observation is an anomaly. Scores closer to 1 are more likely to be an outlier, and scores closer to 0 are considered more normal.

In practice, you need to decide on a threshold to state for each observation whether you expect it to be an outlier. To convert the continuous 0 to 1 scale into a yes/no answer, you use a thresholder.

Constant thresholder

The constant thresholder is the simplest approach that you would intuitively come up with. You will give a constant value that will split observations with a continuous (0 to 1) anomaly score into yes/no anomalies based on being higher or lower than the constant.

As an example, if you specify a value of 0.95 to be your constant threshold, every observation with an anomaly higher than that will be considered an anomaly, and every data point that is scored lower than that is not considered an anomaly.

Quantile thresholder

The quantile thresholder is slightly more advanced. Rather than a constant, you specify a quantile. You have seen quantiles before in the chapter on descriptive statistics. A 0.95 quantile means that 95% of the observations are below this value and 5% of the observations are above it.

Imagine that you used a constant threshold of 0.95, but the model has detected no points above 0.95. In this case, the constant thresholder would split no observations at all into the anomaly class. The quantile thresholder of 0.95 would still give you exactly 5% of your observations as anomalies.

The preferred behavior will depend on your use case, but at least you have the two options at the ready for your anomaly detection in River.

Anomaly detection algorithm 1 – One-Class SVM

Let's now move on to the first anomaly detection algorithm: One-Class SVM. You'll first see a general overview of how One-Class SVM works for anomaly detection. After that, you'll see how it is adapted for an online context in River and you'll do a Python use case using One-Class SVM in Python.

General use of One-Class SVM on anomaly detection

One-Class SVM is an unsupervised outlier detection algorithm based on the **Support Vector Machine (SVM)** classification algorithm.

SVMs are commonly used models for classification or other supervised learning. In supervised learning, they are known to be great for using the kernel trick, which maps the inputs into high-dimensional feature spaces. With this process, SVMs are able to generate non-linear classification.

As described earlier, anomaly detection algorithms need to understand what is normal, but they don't have to understand the non-normal classes. The One-Class SVM is, therefore, an adaptation of the regular SVMs. In regular, supervised SVMs, you need to specify the classes (target variable), but in One-Class SVM, you act like all the data is in a single class.

Basically, the One-Class SVM will just fit an SVM in which it tries to fit a model that best predicts all of the variables as the same target class. When the model fits well, the maximum of individuals will have a low error in their prediction.

Individuals with a high error score for the best-fitting model are difficult to predict using the same model as for the other individuals. You could consider that they may need another model and, therefore, hypothesize that the individuals do not come from the same data-generating process. They may well, therefore, be anomalies.

The error is used as a thresholding score to split individuals. Individuals with a high error score can be classified as anomalies and individuals with a low error score can be considered normal. This split is generally done with a quantile threshold, which was introduced earlier.

Online One-Class SVM in River

The OneClassSVM model in River is described in the documentation as a stochastic implementation of the One-Class SVM and it will not, unfortunately, perfectly match the offline definition of the algorithm. If it is important for your use case to find exact results, you could try out online and offline implementations and see how much they differ.

In general, outlier detection is an unsupervised task, and it is hard to be totally sure about the final answer and precision of your models. This is not a problem as long as you monitor results and take KPI selection and tracking of your business results seriously.

Application on a use case

Let's now apply the online training process of a One-Class SVM using River.

For this example, let's create our own dataset so that we can be sure of the data that should be considered an outlier or not:

1. Let's create a uniform distribution variable with 1,000 observations between 0 and 1:

Code Block 5-4

```
import numpy as np
normal_data = np.random.rand(1000)
```

2. The histogram of the current run can be prepared as follows, but it will change due to randomness:

Code Block 5-5

```
import matplotlib.pyplot as plt
plt.hist(normal_data)
```

The resulting plot will show the following histogram:

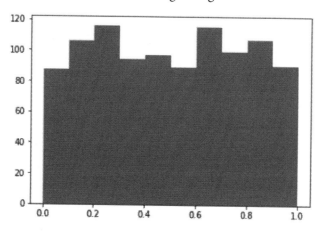

Figure 5.3 – Plot of the normal data

3. As we know this distribution very well, we know what to expect: any data point between 0 and 1 is normal and every data point outside 0 to 1 is an outlier. Let's now add 1% of outliers to the data. Let's make 0.5% of easy-to-detect outliers (random int between 2 and 3 and between -1 and -2), which is very far away from our normal distribution. Let's also make 0.5% of our outliers a bit harder to detect (between 0 and -1 and between 1 and 2).

    This way we can challenge the model and see how well it performs:

Code Block 5-6

```
hard_to_detect = list(np.random.
uniform(1,2,size=int(0.005*1000))) + \
                 list(np.random.uniform(0,-
1,size=int(0.005*1000)))


easy_to_detect = list(np.random.
uniform(2,3,size=int(0.005*1000))) + \
                 list(np.random.uniform(-1,-
2,size=int(0.005*1000)))
```

4. Let's put all that data together and write code to deliver it to the model in a streaming fashion, as follows:

Code Block 5-7

```
total_data = list(normal_data) + hard_to_detect + easy_
to_detect

import random
random.shuffle(total_data)

for datapoint in total_data:
    pass
```

5. Now, the only thing remaining to do is to add the model into the loop:

Code Block 5-8

```
# Anomaly percentage for the quantile thresholder
expected_percentage_anomaly = 20/1020
expected_percentage_normal = 1 - expected_percentage_
anomaly
```

6. Here, you can fit the model:

Code Block 5-9

```
!pip install river
from river import anomaly
model = anomaly.QuantileThresholder(
    anomaly.OneClassSVM(),
    q=expected_percentage_normal
    )


for datapoint in total_data:
    model = model.learn_one({'x': datapoint})
```

When running this code, you have now trained an online One-Class SVM on our synthetic data points!

7. Let's try to get an idea of how well it worked. In this following code, you see how to obtain the scores of each individual and the assignment to the classes:

Code Block 5-10

```
scores = []
for datapoint in total_data:
    scores.append(model.score_one({'x': datapoint}))
```

8. As we know the actual result, we can now compare whether the answers were right. You can use the following code for that:

Code Block 5-11

```
import pandas as pd
results = pd.DataFrame({'data': total_data
, 'score': scores})
results['actual_
outlier'] = (results['data'] > 1 ) | (results
['data'] < 0)


# there are 20 actual outliers
results['actual_outlier'].value_counts()
```

The results are shown here:

```
False    1000
True       20
Name: outlier, dtype: int64
```

Figure 5.4 – The results of Code Block 5-11

9. The following code block will compute the value counts of what the algorithm has detected:

Code Block 5-12

```
# the algo detected 22 outliers
results['score'].value_counts()
```

The following figure shows that 22 outliers were detected:

```
0    998
1     22
Name: score, dtype: int64
```

Figure 5.5 – The results of Code Block 5-12

10. We should now compute how many of the detected outliers are actual outliers and how many are not actual outliers. This is done in the following code block:

Code Block 5-13

```
# in the 22 detected otuliuers,
10 are actual outliers, but 12
are not actually outliers
results.groupby('actual_outlier')
['score'].sum()
```

The result is that out of the 22 detected outliers, 10 are actual outliers, but 12 are not actually outliers. This can be seen in the following figure:

```
actual_outlier
False    12
True     10
Name: score, dtype: int64
```

Figure 5.6 – The results of Code Block 5-13

The obtained result is not too bad: at least some of the outliers were detected correctly, and this could be a good minimum viable product to start automating anomaly detection for this particular use case. Let's see whether we can beat it with a different anomaly detection algorithm!

Anomaly detection algorithm 2 – Half-Space-Trees

The second main anomaly detection algorithm that you'll see here is the online alternative to Isolation Forests, a commonly used and performant outlier detection algorithm.

General use of Isolation Forests in anomaly detection

Isolation Forests work a bit differently than most anomaly detection algorithms. As described throughout this chapter, many models do anomaly detection by first understanding the *normal* data points and then deciding whether a data point is relatively similar to the other normal points or not. If not, it is considered an outlier.

Isolation Forests are a great invention, as they work the other way around. They try to model everything that is not normal, and they try to isolate those points from the rest.

In order to isolate observations, the Isolation Forest will randomly select features and then split the feature between the minimum and the maximum. The number of splits required to isolate a sample is considered a good description of the **isolation score** of an observation.

If it is easy to isolate it (short path to isolation, equivalent to having little splits to isolate the point), then it is probably a relatively isolated data point, and we could class it as an outlier.

How does it change with River?

In River, the model has to train online, and they had to make some adaptations to make it work. The fact that some adaptations have been made is the reason for callling the model `HalfSpaceTrees` in River.

As something to keep in mind, the anomalies have to be spread out in the dataset in order for the model to work well. Also, the model needs all values to be between 0 and 1.

Application of Half-Space-Trees on an anomaly detection use case

We will implement this as follows:

1. Let's now apply Half-Space-Trees to the same, univariate use case and see what happens:

Code Block 5-14

```
from river import anomaly


model2 = anomaly.QuantileThresholder(
    anomaly.HalfSpaceTrees(),
    q=expected_percentage_normal
    )


for datapoint in total_data:
    model2 = model2.learn_one({'x':
 datapoint})
scores2 = []
for datapoint in total_data:
    scores2.append(model2.score_one({'x'
 : datapoint}))


import pandas as pd
results2 = pd.DataFrame({'data': total_
data, 'score': scores2})
results2['actual_outlier'] = (results2
```

```
['data'] > 1 ) | (results2['data'] < 0)


# there are 20 actual outliers
results2['actual_outlier'].value_counts()
```

The results of this code block can be seen in the following figure. It appears that there are 20 actual outliers:

```
False    1000
True       20
Name: actual_outlier, dtype: int64
```

Figure 5.7 – The results of Code Block 5-14

2. You can now compute how many outliers the model detected using the following code:

Code Block 5-15

```
# the algo detected 29 outliers
results2['score'].value_counts()
```

It appears that the algorithm detected 29 outliers. This can be seen in the following figure:

```
0    991
1     29
Name: score, dtype: int64
```

Figure 5.8 – The results of Code Block 5-15

3. We will now compute how many of those 29 detected outliers were actually outliers to see whether our model is any good:

Code Block 5-16

```
# the 29 detected outliers are not actually outliers
results2.groupby('actual_outlier')['score'].sum()
```

The results show that our 29 detected outliers were not really outliers, indicating that this model is not a good choice for this task. There is really no problem with that. After all, this is the exact reason to do model benchmarking:

```
actual_outlier
False    29
True      0
Name: score, dtype: int64
```

Figure 5.9 – The results of Code Block 5-16

As you can see, this model is less performant in the current use case. In conclusion, the One-Class SVM performed better at identifying anomalies in our sample of 1,000 draws of a uniform distribution on the interval 0 to 1.

Going further with anomaly detection

To go further with anomaly detection use cases, you can try out using different datasets or even a dataset of your own use case. As you have seen in the example, data points are inputted as a dictionary. In the current example, you used univariate data points: only one entry in the dictionary.

In practice, you generally have multivariate problems, and you would have multiple variables in your input. Models may be able to fit better in such use cases.

Summary

In this chapter, you have learned how anomaly detection works, both in streaming and non-streaming contexts. This category of machine learning models takes a number of variables about a situation and uses this information to detect whether specific data points or observations are likely to be different from the others.

You have gotten an overview of different use cases for this. Some of those are the monitoring of IT systems, or production line sensor data in manufacturing. Whenever it is problematic to have a data point that is too different from the others, anomaly detection is of great added value.

You have finished the chapter by implementing a model benchmark in which you have benchmarked two online anomaly detection models from the River library. You have seen one model being able to detect a part of the anomalies, and the other model having much worse performances. This has introduced you not only to anomaly detection but also to model benchmarking and model evaluation.

In the next chapter, you will see even more on those topics. You will be working on online classification models, and you will again see how to implement model benchmarking and metrics, but this time, for classification rather than anomaly detection. As you have seen in this chapter, classification can sometimes be used for anomaly detection as well, making the two use cases related to each other.

Further reading

- *Anomaly Detection*: https://en.wikipedia.org/wiki/Anomaly_detection

- *River ML Constant Thresholder*: https://riverml.xyz/latest/api/anomaly/ConstantThresholder/

- *River ML Quantile Thresholder*: https://riverml.xyz/latest/api/anomaly/QuantileThresholder/

- *Support Vector Machine*: https://en.wikipedia.org/wiki/Support-vector_machine

- *Scikit Learn One Class SVM*: https://scikit-learn.org/stable/modules/generated/sklearn.svm.OneClassSVM.html

- *River ML One Class SVM*: https://riverml.xyz/latest/api/anomaly/OneClassSVM/

- *Isolation Forest*: https://en.wikipedia.org/wiki/Isolation_forest

- *River ML Half-Space Trees*: https://riverml.xyz/latest/api/anomaly/HalfSpaceTrees/

6
Online Classification

In the previous two chapters, you were introduced to some basic notions of classification. You first saw a use case in which online classification models in River were used to build a model that can identify an iris species based on a number of characteristics of a plant. This iris dataset is one of the best-known datasets in the world and is a very common starting point for classification.

After that, you looked at anomaly detection. We discussed how classification models can be used for anomaly detection for those cases where we can label anomalies as one class and non-anomalies as another class. Specific anomaly detection models are often better at the task, as they strive to understand only the non-anomalies. Classification models will strive to understand each of the classes.

In this chapter, you'll go much deeper into classification. The chapter will start by posing definitions of what classification is and what it can be used for. You will then see a number of classification models, of which you'll learn the differences between their online and offline counterparts. You will also implement multiple examples in Python using the River package. This will, in the end, result in a model benchmarking study for the use case that will be introduced later on.

This chapter will cover the following topics:

- Defining classification
- Identifying use cases of classification
- Classification algorithms in River

Technical requirements

You can find all the code for this book on GitHub at the following link: `https://github.com/PacktPublishing/Machine-Learning-for-Streaming-Data-with-Python`. If you are not yet familiar with Git and GitHub, the easiest way to download the notebooks and code samples is the following:

1. Go to the link of the repository.

2. Click the green **Code** button.

3. Select **Download ZIP**.

When you download the ZIP file, unzip it in your local environment, and you will be able to access the code through your preferred Python editor.

Python environment

To follow along with this book, you can download the code in the repository and execute it using your preferred Python editor.

If you are not yet familiar with Python environments, I would advise you to check out Anaconda (`https://www.anaconda.com/products/individual`), which comes with Jupyter Notebook and JupyterLab, which are both great for executing notebooks. It also comes with Spyder and VSCode for editing scripts and programs.

If you have difficulty installing Python or the associated programs on your machine, you can check out Google Colab (`https://colab.research.google.com/`) or Kaggle Notebooks (`https://www.kaggle.com/code`), which both allow you to run Python code in online notebooks for free, without any setup to do.

Defining classification

In this chapter, you will discover classification. Classification is a supervised machine learning task in which a model is constructed that assigns observations to a category.

The simplest types of classification models that everybody tends to know are decision trees. Let's consider a super simple example of how a decision tree could be used for classification.

Imagine that we have a dataset in which we have observations about five humans and five animals. The goal is to use this data to build a decision tree that can be used on any new, unseen animal or human.

The data can be imported as follows:

Code Block 6-1

```
import pandas as pd

# example to classify human vs animal

#dataset with one variable
can_speak = [True,True,True,True,True,True,True,False,False,False]
has_feathers = [False,False,False,False,False,True,True,False,
False,False]
is_human =
[True,True,True,True,True,False,False,False,False,False]


data = pd.DataFrame({'can_speak': can_speak, 'has_feathers':
has_feathers, 'is_human': is_human})
data
```

The data is shown in the following figure:

	can_speak	has_feathers	is_human
0	True	False	True
1	True	False	True
2	True	False	True
3	True	False	True
4	True	False	True
5	True	True	False
6	True	True	False
7	False	False	False
8	False	False	False
9	False	False	False

Figure 6.1 – The data

Now, to construct the decision tree, you would generally use machine learning, as that is far more efficient than constructing the tree by hand. Yet, for this example, let's do a simple decision tree that works as the following graph indicates:

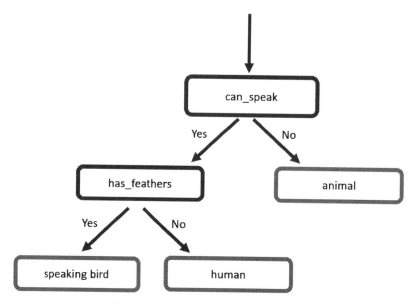

Figure 6.2 – The example decision tree

Of course, this is a model, so it is only a partial representation of the truth. It works quite well for the current dataset of 10 observations, but with more data points, you would encounter all types of anomalies, so you'd need more variables.

You could code this model for a human versus not human classification in Python as follows:

Code Block 6-2

```
def self_made_decision_tree(observation):
    if observation.can_speak:
        if not observation.has_feathers:
            return 'human'


    return 'not human'


for i,row in data.iterrows():
    print(self_made_decision_tree(row))
```

The result is the following:

```
human
human
human
human
human
not human
not human
not human
not human
not human
```

Figure 6.3 – The predicted outcomes

The general idea behind this is that a classification model is any machine learning model that uses the data to generate decision rules to assign observations to specific classes. In the next section, we'll be going into some use cases of classification to get a better idea of what it can be used for in practice.

Identifying use cases of classification

The use cases of classification are huge; it is a very commonly used method in many projects. Still, let's see some examples to get a better idea of the different types of use cases that can benefit from classification methods.

Use case 1 – email spam classification

The first use case that is generally built on classification is **spam detection** in email. Spam emails have been around for a long time. The business model of sending fake emails to generally steal people's money is a big problem, and receiving many spam emails can negatively impact your emailing experience.

Email service providers have come a long way in detecting spam emails automatically and sending them to your spam/junk box. Nowadays, this is all done automatically and relies heavily on machine learning.

If you compare this to our super-small classification example, you could imagine that the decision tree (or any other model) can take several information types about every received email and use that to decide whether or not the email should be classified as spam. This has to be done in real time, as nobody wants to wait for a spam detection service to finally send their email through.

You can read more about this use case in the following resources:

- `https://www.sciencedirect.com/science/article/pii/S2405844018353404`

- `https://www.enjoyalgorithms.com/blog/email-spam-and-non-spam-filtering-using-machine-learning`

Use case 2 – face detection in phone camera

The second example of classification is face detection when you want to unlock your phone. Your phone has to make a split-second decision whether the face it's seeing is the face of its owner or not.

This decision is a classification decision, as it comes down to a yes/no decision: it *is* the owner, or it is *not* the owner. This decision will generally be made by machine learning, as the rules would be very complex and hard to write down as `if/else` statements. Machine learning algorithms are, nowadays, relatively good at such use cases.

For other more detailed examples of this use case, you can check out the following links:

- `https://www.xfinity.com/hub/mobile/facial-recognition-on-phone`

- `https://www.nytimes.com/wirecutter/blog/how-facial-recognition-works/`

Use case 3 – online marketing ad selection

A final example to add to the previous two is online marketing ad selection. Many websites nowadays display personalized ads. This means that you will see an advertisement that matches you as a customer.

Personalized ad systems do not invent ads though; they have to make a decision and choose between multiple available ads to know which one fits you best. In this way, it is a classification, as it has to decide between multiple choices.

As you can understand, page loads have to be fast and, therefore, ad selection has to be done in a split second as well. Real-time responses are key for the model to provide any value at all.

The following links talk in more depth about this use case:

- `https://www.owox.com/blog/articles/machine-learning-in-marketing/`
- `https://www.ibm.com/watson-advertising/thought-leadership/benefits-of-machine-learning-in-advertising`

In the next section, you'll see a more practical side to doing classification, as you will discover several classification algorithms in the River Python library.

Overview of classification algorithms in River

There is a large number of online classification models available in the River online machine learning package.

A selection of relevant ones is as follows:

- `LogisticRegression`
- `Perceptron`
- `AdaptiveRandomForestClassifier`
- `ALMAClassifier`
- `PAClassifier`

Classification algorithm 1 – LogisticRegression

Logistic regression is one of the most basic statistical classification models. It models a dependent variable (target variable) that has two classes (1 or 0) and can use multiple independent variables to make the prediction.

The model combines each of the independent variables as log-odds; you can see this as the coefficients in linear regression, except that they are log-odds for each variable. The split in the model is based on the logistic function.

You can see a simplified schematic of the idea as follows:

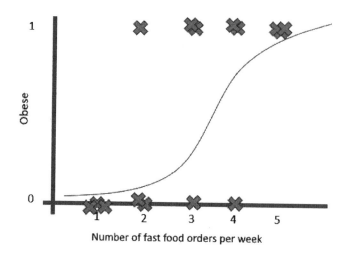

Figure 6.4 – The logistic curve

Logistic regression in River

For online logistic regression, you can use the `LogisticRegression` class in River's `linear_model` section. Let's now see an example of that:

1. First, you can start by making a classification dataset using sklearn's inbuilt `make_blobs` function, which makes classification datasets. You can use the following code for this:

Code Block 6-3

```
from sklearn.datasets import make _ blobs
X,y=make _ blobs(shuffle=True,centers=2,n _ samples=2000)
```

2. To see what this dataset looks like, it is important to make a plot. You can use the following `matplotlib` code for this:

Code Block 6-4

```
import matplotlib.pyplot as plt
plt.scatter(X[:,0], X[:,1], c=y)
```

You should obtain the following plot, or something resembling it:

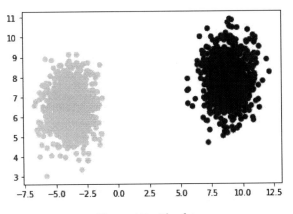

Figure 6.5 – The data

3. To make sure that your model evaluation will be fair, it is important to make a train-test split in the data. You can do this with sklearn's `train_test_split`, as shown here:

Code Block 6-5

```
from sklearn.model_selection import train_test_split
X_train, X_test, y_train, y_test = train_test_split(X, y, test_size=0.33, random_state=42)
```

4. Let's now move on to the application of the logistic regression model. The following code shows how to fit the model one data point at a time. Note that you should be using a JSON conversion of the input data for x, as this is required by River:

Code Block 6-6

```
!pip install river
from river import linear_model


model=linear_model.LogisticRegression()


for x_i,y_i in zip(X_train,y_train):
    x_json = {'val1': x_i[0], 'val2': x_i[1]}
    print(x_json, y_i)
    model.learn_one(x_json,y_i)
```

The printed data will look something like this:

```
{'val1': -4.704663864297298, 'val2': 6.1003283246794755} 1
{'val1': -4.680729582785402, 'val2': 6.414576161192015} 1
{'val1': 8.64377655745292, 'val2': 8.092691356714708} 0
{'val1': -2.514498848183771, 'val2': 7.058169410417593} 1
{'val1': -5.21378558855869, 'val2': 5.940715469387418} 1
{'val1': 7.840402787542638, 'val2': 8.75992081155734} 0
{'val1': 8.650143833239868, 'val2': 5.207336179827417} 0
{'val1': -5.1205343899694755, 'val2': 7.3360340844401122} 1
{'val1': -2.0995583922573324, 'val2': 5.804757772906635} 1
{'val1': 8.791489583147516, 'val2': 9.177436606115824} 0
{'val1': 10.104169014992802, 'val2': 8.817858841282048} 0
{'val1': -4.959066997983176, 'val2': 6.168425965580823} 1
{'val1': -3.3418322777762692, 'val2': 4.627361050980675} 1
{'val1': 9.744134402569214, 'val2': 7.339671588458472} 0
{'val1': -3.388418866591099, 'val2': 7.494427621828238} 1
{'val1': -2.0741796728295383, 'val2': 6.875266157180873} 1
{'val1': -4.744917558314091, 'val2': 7.185438529887843} 1
{'val1': 8.586109522227948, 'val2': 6.565731138178554} 0
{'val1': 9.32225460102962, 'val2': 8.513182006941472} 0
```

Figure 6.6 – The output of Code Block 6-6

5. You can do predictions one by one as well, or you can use `predict_many` to make all the predictions on the test set at once. There will not be any difference in the result. In the following code, `predict_many` is used:

Code Block 6-7

```
import pandas as pd
preds = model.predict _ many(pd.DataFrame(X _
test,columns=['val1', 'val2']))
```

6. To get a quality metric on this prediction, let's use the accuracy score by `scikit-learn`. As you can see in the following code block, the model has obtained 100% accuracy on the blob data example. It must be stated that this blob data example is a simple prediction task as the data is perfectly separable by a straight line, as can be seen in the plot shown earlier:

Code Block 6-8

```
from sklearn.metrics import accuracy _ score
accuracy _ score(y _ test, preds)
```

This should result in the following output:

$$Out[123]:\ \textbf{1.0}$$

Figure 6.7 – The output of Code Block 6-8

Classification algorithm 2 – Perceptron

The perceptron is another algorithm for supervised learning on classification problems. It takes inputs, multiplies them by weights, and puts the sum of those through an activation function. The output is the resulting classification. The following graph shows an example:

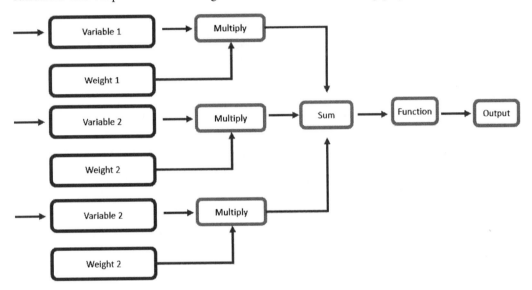

Figure 6.8 – Schematic overview of a perceptron

Perceptron in River

Like logistic regression, the perceptron is a commonly used offline model that has been reworked into an online model for River. In River, the perceptron has been implemented as a special case of logistic regression.

You can use the perceptron just like logistic regression. You can use the same code example as in the previous case, as follows:

Code Block 6-9

```
# make data
from sklearn.datasets import make_blobs
X,y=make_blobs(shuffle=True,centers=2,n_samples=2000)
```

```
# train test split
from sklearn.model_selection import train_test_split
X_train, X_test, y_train, y_test = train_test_split(X, y,
test_size=0.33, random_state=42)


# build the model
from river import linear_model
model=linear_model.Perceptron()


# fit the model
for x_i,y_i in zip(X_train,y_train):
    x_json = {'val1': x_i[0], 'val2': x_i[1]}
    model.learn_one(x_json,y_i)


# predict on the test set
import pandas as pd
preds = model.predict_many(pd.DataFrame(X_test,columns=['val1',
'val2']))


# compute accuracy
from sklearn.metrics import accuracy_score
accuracy_score(y_test, preds)
```

The result is 1.0, which is, unsurprisingly, the same as the logistic regression result.

Classification algorithm 3 – AdaptiveRandomForestClassifier

In the introduction, you already saw the general idea behind a decision tree. Random Forests are an ensemble model that improves decision trees.

The idea behind Random Forests is that they reduce the error of single decision trees by making a large number of slightly different decision trees. The most common prediction among a large number of decision trees is retained as the final prediction.

The decision trees are made slightly differently by fitting each of them on a slightly different dataset, which is created by resampling the observations. There is also a subset of variables used for creating the decision tree splits.

Random Forest in River

For online learning, the data needs to be fitted one by one into the Random Forest, which is not an easy task. River's implementation is based on the two key elements of Random Forests, which are the resampling and the variable subsets. They have also added drift detection for each single decision tree:

1. Let's use an alternative data creation function, which creates data that is harder to separate than the blobs. This function from `sklearn` is called `make_classification`:

Code Block 6-10

```
# make data
from sklearn.datasets import make_classification
X,y=make_classification(shuffle=True,n_samples=2000)


pd.DataFrame(X).head()
```

The data is shown in the following figure:

	0	1	2	3	4	5	6	7	8	9	10
0	-1.889154	0.100780	0.443435	-0.737850	1.019484	0.234298	0.957744	-2.554736	-0.035488	0.493334	-0.215918
1	0.087453	1.289539	0.488679	0.575077	-1.203410	0.252346	0.256476	2.032289	1.378394	-1.388067	-0.540444
2	-1.218000	0.172650	0.734155	1.895608	-0.872459	0.434568	0.356758	0.392302	-1.747061	-0.775751	-1.063004
3	0.781740	1.796209	-1.046414	-0.167494	0.952206	-0.594579	0.699985	-0.426309	-0.773376	1.154559	0.658364
4	-3.876519	-1.642646	-0.905938	0.283973	0.658389	-0.550836	1.860633	0.641810	-0.242383	1.355729	0.769342

Figure 6.9 – The new data

2. There is a total of 20 variables generated by default, of which a number are automatically made more relevant and some are mostly irrelevant. Let's do a train-test split just like before:

Code Block 6-11

```
# train test split
from sklearn.model_selection import train_test_split
X_train, X_test, y_train, y_test = train_test_split(X, y, test_size=0.33, random_state=42)
```

3. Using this train-test split, we can move on to building the model:

Code Block 6-12

```
from river import ensemble
model = ensemble.AdaptiveRandomForestClassifier()

# fit the model
for x_i,y_i in zip(X_train,y_train):
    x_json = {'val'+str(i): x for i,x in enumerate(x_i)}
    model.learn_one(x_json,y_i)
```

4. Now that the model is fit, we can make predictions on the test set. There is no predict_many function here, so it is necessary to do a loop with predict_one repeatedly:

Code Block 6-13

```
# predict on the test set
import pandas as pd
preds = []
for x_i in X_test:
    x_json = {'val'+str(i): x for i,x in enumerate(x_i)}
    preds.append(model.predict_one(x_json))
```

5. As a final step, let's compute the accuracy of this model:

Code Block 6-14

```
# compute accuracy
from sklearn.metrics import accuracy_score
accuracy_score(y_test, preds)
```

6. The result is 0.86. Of course, the dataset was more difficult to predict, so that is not to be mistaken for a bad score. As an additional metric, we can look at the classification report for more information:

Code Block 6-15

```
# classification report
from sklearn.metrics import classification_report
print(classification_report(y_test, preds))
```

The result is shown in the following figure:

	precision	recall	f1-score	support
0	0.87	0.86	0.87	328
1	0.86	0.87	0.87	332
accuracy			0.87	660
macro avg	0.87	0.87	0.87	660
weighted avg	0.87	0.87	0.87	660

Figure 6.10 – The output of Code Block 6-15

In this classification report, you see that the precision and recall and the scores for positives and negatives are all relatively equal. This shows that there is no imbalance in the classifier, which is important when relying on the accuracy score.

Classification algorithm 4 – ALMAClassifier

Now that you have seen some commonly used machine learning models for classification in a way adapted to accommodate online learning, it is time to see some more specific models as well. The first of these is the ALMA classifier.

The **approximate large margin algorithm (ALMA)** classifier is an incremental implementation of **support vector machines (SVMs)**, a commonly used machine learning model for classification.

You saw the adaptation of SVMs in the previous chapter: a one-class SVM is often used for anomaly detection. For classification, you'd use a regular (two-class) SVM.

ALMAClassifier in River

Let's see how ALMAClassifier compares to the adaptive Random Forest, by executing it on the same data:

1. We start by applying the same code that we already defined before:

Code Block 6-16

```
# make data
from sklearn.datasets import make_classification
X,y=make_classification(shuffle=True,n_samples=2000)
# train test split
from sklearn.model_selection import train_test_split
X_train, X_test, y_train, y_test = train_test_
split(X, y, test_size=0.33, random_state=42)
from river import linear_model
model = linear_model.ALMAClassifier()
# fit the model
for x_i,y_i in zip(X_train,y_train):
    x_json = {'val'+str(i): x for i,x in enumerate(x_i)}
    model.learn_one(x_json,y_i)
# predict on the test set
import pandas as pd
preds = []
for x_i in X_test:
    x_json = {'val'+str(i): x for i,x in enumerate(x_i)}
    preds.append(model.predict_one(x_json))
# compute accuracy
from sklearn.metrics import accuracy_score
accuracy_score(y_test, preds)
```

2. The result is 0.77, not as good as the Random Forest. Let's also check the classification report to see whether anything changed there:

Code Block 6-17

```
# classification report
from sklearn.metrics import classification_report
print(classification_report(y_test, preds))
```

3. The result is shown in the following figure:

	precision	recall	f1-score	support
0	0.80	0.75	0.77	331
1	0.76	0.81	0.78	329
accuracy			0.78	660
macro avg	0.78	0.78	0.78	660
weighted avg	0.78	0.78	0.78	660

Figure 6.11 – The output of Code Block 6-17

There is a little more variation here, but nothing that seems too shocking. In general, the Random Forest was just better overall for this data.

Classification algorithm 5 – PAClassifier

The **passive-aggressive (PA)** classifier is an online machine learning model that is not related to any existing offline model. It is based on the idea of updating the model at each step and thereby solving the following problem:

The update of the classifier is performed by solving a constrained optimization problem: we would like the new classifier to remain as close as possible to the current one while achieving at least a unit margin on the most recent example.

This quote has been taken from the following paper on PA algorithms, which is also an interesting reference for further reading: https://jmlr.csail.mit.edu/papers/volume7/crammer06a/crammer06a.pdf.

The name *passive-aggressive* comes from the idea that an algorithm that learns too quickly from each new data point is considered too aggressive. PA is less aggressive.

PAClassifier in River

Let's see how the PA classifier performs on the same task as the two previous models:

Code Block 6-18

```
# make data
from sklearn.datasets import make_classification
X,y=make_classification(shuffle=True,n_samples=2000)
# train test split
from sklearn.model_selection import train_test_split
X_train, X_test, y_train, y_test = train_test_split(X, y,
test_size=0.33, random_state=42)
```

```
from river import linear_model
model = linear_model.PAClassifier()
# fit the model
for x_i,y_i in zip(X_train,y_train):
    x_json = {'val'+str(i): x for i,x in enumerate(x_i)}
    model.learn_one(x_json,y_i)
# predict on the test set
import pandas as pd
preds = []
for x_i in X_test:
    x_json = {'val'+str(i): x for i,x in enumerate(x_i)}
    preds.append(model.predict_one(x_json))
# compute accuracy
from sklearn.metrics import accuracy_score
accuracy_score(y_test, preds)
```

The obtained score is 0.85. The following section summarizes all the scores that we have obtained.

Evaluating benchmark results

This leaves us with the following accuracy scores for the past three models:

Models	Accuracy Score
AdaptiveRandomForest	0.866
ALMAClassifier	0.77
PAClassifier	0.856

Table 6.1 – The table with the results

The best result was obtained by AdaptiveRandomForest and PAClassifier came in second place. ALMAClassifier was less performant with a score of 0.77.

Summary

In this chapter, you have first seen a general overview of classification and its use cases. You have understood how it is different from anomaly detection, but how it can sometimes still be applied to anomaly detection use cases.

You have learned about five models for online classification of which some are mainly adaptations of offline models, and others are specifically designed for working in an online manner. Both types exist, and it is important to have the tools to benchmark model performance before making a choice for a final model.

The model benchmark that you executed in Python was done in such a way as to find the best model in terms of the accuracy of the model on a test set. You have seen clear differences between the benchmarked models, and this is a great showcase for the importance of model benchmarking.

In the following chapter, you will do the same type of model benchmarking exercise, but this time, you will be focusing on a regression use case, which has a goal that is fundamentally different from classification. This comes with some changes with respect to measuring errors and benchmarking, but from a high-level perspective, also has a lot in common with the classification benchmarking use case that you worked with in this chapter.

Further reading

- *LogisticRegression*: `https://riverml.xyz/latest/api/linear-model/LogisticRegression/`
- *Perceptron*: `https://riverml.xyz/latest/api/linear-model/Perceptron/`
- *AdaptiveRandomForestClassifier*: `https://riverml.xyz/latest/api/ensemble/AdaptiveRandomForestClassifier/`
- *ALMA*: `https://riverml.xyz/latest/api/linear-model/ALMAClassifier/`
- *ALMA*: `https://www.jmlr.org/papers/volume2/gentile01a/gentile01a.pdf`
- *PAClassifier*: `https://riverml.xyz/latest/api/linear-model/PAClassifier/`
- *PAClassifier*: `https://jmlr.csail.mit.edu/papers/volume7/crammer06a/crammer06a.pdf`
- *make_classification*: `https://scikit-learn.org/stable/modules/generated/sklearn.datasets.make_classification.htm`
- *make_blobs*: `https://scikit-learn.org/stable/modules/generated/sklearn.datasets.make_blobs.html`

7
Online Regression

After looking at online anomaly detection and online classification throughout the previous chapters, there is one large category of online machine learning that remains to be seen. **Regression** is the family of supervised machine learning models that applies to use cases in which the target variable is numerical.

In anomaly detection and classification, you have seen how to build models to predict categorical targets (yes/no and iris species), but you have not yet seen how to work with a target that is numerical. Working with numerical data requires having methods that work differently, both in the deeper layers of model training and model definition and also in our use of metrics.

Imagine being a weather forecaster trying to forecast the temperature (Celsius) for tomorrow. Maybe you expect a sunny day, and you have a model that you use to predict a temperature of 25 degrees Celsius. Imagine if the next day, you observe that it is cold and only 18 degrees; you were clearly wrong.

Now, imagine that you predicted 24 degrees. In a classification use case, you may tend to say that 25 is not 24, so the result is wrong. However, the result of 24 is *less wrong* than the result of 18.

In regression, one single prediction can be more or less wrong. In practice, you will rarely be entirely right. In classification, you are either wrong or right, so this is different. This introduces a need for new metrics and a change in the model benchmarking process.

In this chapter, you will first get a deeper introduction to regression models, focusing on online regression models in River. After that, you'll be working on a regression model benchmark.

This chapter covers the following topics:

- Defining regression
- Use cases of regression
- Overview of regression algorithms in River

Technical requirements

You can find all the code for this book on GitHub at the following link: `https://github.com/PacktPublishing/Machine-Learning-for-Streaming-Data-with-Python`. If you are not yet familiar with Git and GitHub, the easiest way to download the notebooks and code samples is the following:

1. Go to the link of the repository.
2. Go to the green **Code** button.
3. Select **Download ZIP**.

When you download the ZIP file, unzip it in your local environment, and you will be able to access the code through your preferred Python editor.

Python environment

To follow along with this book, you can download the code in the repository and execute it using your preferred Python editor.

If you are not yet familiar with Python environments, I would advise you to check out Anaconda (`https://www.anaconda.com/products/individual`), which comes with Jupyter Notebook and JupyterLab, which are both great for executing notebooks. It also comes with Spyder and VS Code for editing scripts and programs.

If you have difficulty installing Python or the associated programs on your machine, you can check out Google Colab (`https://colab.research.google.com/`) or Kaggle Notebooks (`https://www.kaggle.com/code`), which both allow you to run Python code in online notebooks for free, without any setup required.

Defining regression

In this chapter, you will discover regression. Regression is a supervised machine learning task in which a model is constructed that predicts or estimates a numerical target variable based on numerical or categorical independent variables.

The simplest type of regression model is **linear regression**. Let's consider a super simple example of how a linear regression could be used for regression.

Imagine that we have a dataset in which we have observations of 10 people. Based on the number of hours they study per week, we have to estimate their average grade (on a 1 to 10 scale). Of course, this is a strongly oversimplified problem.

The data looks as follows:

Code Block 7-1

```
import pandas as pd
nb_hrs_studies = [1, 2, 3, 4, 5, 6, 7, 8, 9, 10]
avg_grade = [5.5, 5.8, 6.8, 7.2, 7.4, 7.8, 8.2, 8.8, 9.3, 9.4]
data = pd.DataFrame({'nb_hrs_studies': nb_hrs_studies, 'avg_
grade': avg_grade})
data
```

You will obtain the following data frame:

	nb_hrs_studies	avg_grade
0	1	5.5
1	2	5.8
2	3	6.8
3	4	7.2
4	5	7.4
5	6	7.8
6	7	8.2
7	8	8.8
8	9	9.3
9	10	9.4

Figure 7.1 – The dataset

Let's plot the data to see how this can be made into a regression problem:

Code Block 7-2

```
import matplotlib.pyplot as plt
plt.scatter(data['nb_hrs_studies'], data['avg_grade'])
plt.xlabel('nb_hrs_studies')
plt.ylabel('avg_grades')
```

This results in the following output:

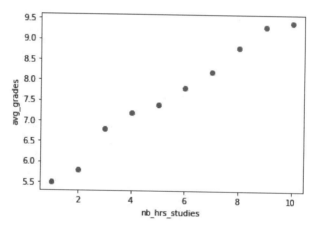

Figure 7.2 – A scatter plot of the data

Now, the goal of linear regression is to fit the line (or hyperplane) that best goes through these points and is able to predict an estimated `avg_grades` for any `nb_hrs_studies`. Other regression models each have their specific way to construct the prediction function, but eventually have the same goal: creating the best fitting formula to predict a numerical target variable using one or more independent variables.

In the next section, you'll discover some example use cases in which regression can be used.

Use cases of regression

The use cases of regression are huge: it is a very commonly used method in many projects. Still, let's see some examples to get a better idea of the different types of use cases that can benefit from regression models.

Use case 1 – Forecasting

A very common use case for regression algorithms is forecasting. In forecasting, the goal is to predict future values of a variable that is measured over time. Such variables are called **time series**. Although a number of specific methods exist for time series modeling, regression models are also great contenders for obtaining good performance on future prediction performance.

In some forecasting use cases, real-time responses are very important. An example is stock trading, in which the datapoints of stock prices arrive at a huge velocity and forecasts have to be adapted straight away to use the best possible information for stock trades. Even automated stock trading algorithms exist, and they need to react fast in order to make the most profit on their trades as possible.

For further reading on this topic, you could start by checking out the following links:

- https://www.investopedia.com/articles/financial-theory/09/regression-analysis-basics-business.asp
- https://www.mathworks.com/help/econ/time-series-regression-vii-forecasting.html

Use case 2 – Predicting the number of faulty products in manufacturing

The second example of real-time and streaming regression models being used in practice is the application of predictive maintenance models in manufacturing. For example, you could use a real-time prediction of the number of faulty products per hour in a production line. This would be a regression model as well, as the outcome is a number rather than a categorical variable.

The production line could use this prediction for a real-time alerting system, for example, once a threshold of faulty products is predicted to be reached. Real-time data integration is important for this, as having the wrong products being produced is a large waste of resources.

The following two resources will allow you to read more about this use case:

- https://www.sciencedirect.com/science/article/pii/S2405896316308084
- https://www.researchgate.net/publication/315855789_Regression_Models_for_Lean_Production

Now that we have explored some use cases of regression, let's get started with the various algorithms that we have for regression.

Overview of regression algorithms in River

There is a large number of online regression models available in the River online machine learning package.

A selection of relevant ones are as follows:

- `LinearRegression`
- `HoeffdingAdaptiveTreeRegressor`
- `SGTRegressor`
- `SRPRegressor`

Regression algorithm 1 – LinearRegression

Linear regression is one of the most basic regression models. A simple linear regression is a regression model that fits a straight line through the datapoints. The following graph illustrates this:

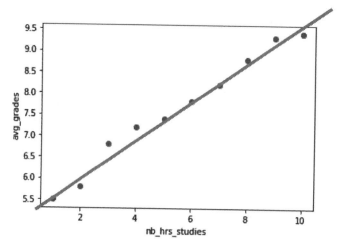

Figure 7.3 – A linear model in a scatter plot

This orange line is a result of the following formula:

$$y = ax + b$$

Here, y represents avg_grades and x represents nb_hrs_studies. When fitting the model, the a and b coefficients are estimates. The b coefficient in this formula is called the intercept. It indicates the value of y when x equals 0. The a coefficient represents the slope of the line. For each additional step in x, a indicates the amount that is added to y.

This is a version of linear regression, but there is also a version called **multiple linear regression**, in which there are multiple x variables. In this case, the model does not represent a line but rather a hyperplane, in which a slope coefficient is added for each additional x variable.

Linear regression in River

Let's now move on to build an example of online linear regression using River ML in Python:

1. If you remember from the previous example, we used a function called make_classification from scikit-learn. The same can be done for regression problems using make_regression:

Code Block 7-3

```
from sklearn.datasets import make_regression
X,y = make_regression(n_samples=1000,n_features=5,n_
informative=5,noise=100)
```

2. To get a better idea of what has resulted from this make_regression function, let's inspect X of this dataset. You can use the following code to get a quick overview of the data:

Code Block 7-4

```
pd.DataFrame(X).describe()
```

The `describe()` method will put out a data frame with descriptive statistics of the variables, as follows:

	0	1	2	3	4
count	1000.000000	1000.000000	1000.000000	1000.000000	1000.000000
mean	-0.001842	0.012383	0.018666	0.023975	-0.034544
std	0.983398	0.954646	0.964876	0.997626	1.016249
min	-3.727848	-2.841878	-3.889398	-2.570243	-3.305025
25%	-0.672259	-0.592181	-0.613667	-0.652700	-0.775806
50%	0.030133	-0.004149	0.018006	-0.004273	-0.039427
75%	0.665840	0.646376	0.683272	0.670445	0.673714
max	2.481220	3.445365	3.507887	2.881402	3.800007

Figure 7.4 – Descriptive statistics

There are five columns in the X data, and there are 1,000 observations.

3. Now, to look at the y variable, also called the `target` variable, we can make a histogram as follows:

Code Block 7-5

```
pd.Series(y).hist()
```

The resulting histogram can be seen in the following figure:

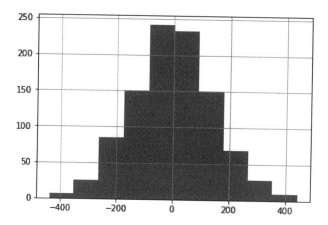

Figure 7.5 – The resulting histogram

There is much more exploratory data analysis that could be done here, but that would be out of scope for this book.

4. Let's now move on to the creation of a train and test set to create a fair model validation approach. In the following code, you can see how to create the train_test_split function from scikit-learn to create a train-test split:

Code Block 7-6

```
from sklearn.model_selection import train_test_split
X_train, X_test, y_train, y_test = train_test_split(X, y,
test_size=0.33, random_state=42)
```

5. You can create the linear regression in River using the following code:

Code Block 7-7

```
!pip install river
from river.linear_model import LinearRegression
model = LinearRegression()
```

6. This model then has to be fitted to the training data. We use the same loop as you have seen earlier on in the book. This loop goes through the individual datapoints (X and y) and converts the X values into a dictionary, as required by River. The model is then updated datapoint by datapoint using the learn_one method:

Code Block 7-8

```
# fit the model
for x_i,y_i in zip(X_train,y_train):
    x_json = {'val'+str(i): x for i,x in enumerate(x_i)}
    model.learn_one(x_json,y_i)
```

7. Once the model has learned from the training data, it needs to be evaluated on the test set. This can be done by looping through the test data and making a prediction for the X values of each datapoint. The y values are stored in a list for evaluation against the actual y values of the test dataset:

Code Block 7-9

```
# predict on the test set
import pandas as pd
```

```
preds = []
for x_i in X_test:
    x_json = {'val'+str(i): x for i,x in enumerate(x_i)}
    preds.append(model.predict_one(x_json))
```

8.   We can now compute the metric of our choice for this regression model, for example, the r2 score. This can be done using the following code:

Code Block 7-10

```
# compute accuracy
from sklearn.metrics import r2_score
r2_score(y_test, preds)
```

The obtained result is 0.478.

Let's find out whether other models are more performant at this task in the next section.

Regression algorithm 2 – HoeffdingAdaptiveTreeRegressor

The second online regression model that we'll cover is a much more specific model for online regression. Whereas the LinearRegression model, just like many other models, is an online adaptation of an essentially offline model, many other models are developed specifically for online models. HoeffdingAdaptiveTreeRegressor is one of those.

The **Hoeffding Adaptive Tree regressor (HATR)** is a regression model that is based on the **Hoeffding Adaptive Tree Classifier (HATC)**. HATC is a tree-based model that uses the **adaptive windowing (ADWIN)** methodology to monitor the performance of the different branches of a tree. The HATC methodology replaces the branches with new branches when their time is due. This is determined by observing the better performance of the new branches by the old branches. HATC is also available in River.

The HATR regression version is based on the HATC approach and uses an ADWIN concept-drift detector at each decision node. This allows the method to detect possible changes in the underlying data, which is called **drift**. Drift detection will be covered in more detail in a further chapter.

HoeffdingAdaptiveTreeRegressor in River

We will check out an example as follows:

1. Let's get started with fitting the model on the same data as we used in the previous model:

Code Block 7-11

```
from river.tree import HoeffdingAdaptiveTreeRegressor
model = HoeffdingAdaptiveTreeRegressor(seed=42)


# fit the model
for x_i,y_i in zip(X_train,y_train):
    x_json = {'val'+str(i): x for i,x in enumerate(x_i)}
    model.learn_one(x_json,y_i)


# predict on the test set
import pandas as pd
preds = []
for x_i in X_test:
    x_json = {'val'+str(i): x for i,x in enumerate(x_i)}
    preds.append(model.predict_one(x_json))


# compute accuracy
from sklearn.metrics import r2_score
r2_score(y_test, preds)
```

2. This model obtains an r2 score that is a little worse than the linear regression: 0.437. Let's see if we can do something to make it work better. Let's write a grid search to see whether a number of hyperparameters can help to improve the model.

   For this, let's write the model as a function that takes values for the hyperparameters and that returns the r2 score:

Code Block 7-12

```
def evaluate_HATR(grace_period, leaf_prediction, model_
selector_decay):
    # model pipeline
    model = (
```

```
        HoeffdingAdaptiveTreeRegressor(
            grace_period=grace_period,
            leaf_prediction=leaf_prediction,
            model_selector_decay=model_selector_decay,
            seed=42)
    )
    # fit the model
    for x_i,y_i in zip(X_train,y_train):
        x_json = {'val'+str(i): x for i,x in
enumerate(x_i)}
        model.learn_one(x_json,y_i)
    # predict on the test set
    preds = []
    for x_i in X_test:
        x_json = {'val'+str(i): x for i,x in
enumerate(x_i)}
        preds.append(model.predict_one(x_json))
    # compute accuracy
    return r2_score(y_test, preds)
```

3. Let's specify the hyperparameters to tune as follows:

Code Block 7-13

```
grace_periods=[0,5,10,]
leaf_predictions=['mean','adaptive']
model_selector_decays=[ 0.3,  0.8,   0.95]
```

4. We then loop through the data as follows:

Code Block 7-14

```
results = []
i = 0
for grace_period in grace_periods:
    for leaf_prediction in leaf_predictions:
        for model_selector_decay in model_selector_
decays:
            print(i)
```

```
            i = i+1
            results.append([grace_period, leaf_
  prediction, model_selector_decay,evaluate_HATR(grace_
  period, leaf_prediction, model_selector_decay)])
```

5. The results can then be obtained as follows:

Code Block 7-15

```
  pd.DataFrame(results, columns=['grace_period', 'leaf_
  prediction', 'model_selector_decay', 'r2_score' ]).sort_
  values('r2_score', ascending=False)
```

The obtained result is slightly disappointing, as none of the tested values were able
to generate a better result. Unfortunately, this is part of data science, as not all
models work well on each use case.

	grace_period	leaf_prediction	model_selector_decay	r2_score
11	5	adaptive	0.95	0.437291
5	0	adaptive	0.95	0.435681
9	5	adaptive	0.30	0.378858
10	5	adaptive	0.80	0.370474
17	10	adaptive	0.95	0.366986
4	0	adaptive	0.80	0.327362
16	10	adaptive	0.80	0.327224
15	10	adaptive	0.30	0.299245
3	0	adaptive	0.30	0.268240
6	5	mean	0.30	0.133708
7	5	mean	0.80	0.133708
8	5	mean	0.95	0.133708
1	0	mean	0.80	0.127751
2	0	mean	0.95	0.127751
0	0	mean	0.30	0.127751
12	10	mean	0.30	0.069420
13	10	mean	0.80	0.069420
14	10	mean	0.95	0.069420

Figure 7.6 – The resulting output of Code Block 7-15

Let's move on to the next model and see whether it fits better.

Regression algorithm 3 – SGTRegressor

SGTRegressor is a stochastic gradient tree for regression. It is another decision tree-based model that can learn with new data arriving. It is an incremental decision tree that minimizes the mean squared error by minimizing the loss function.

SGTRegressor in River

We'll check this out using the following example:

1. Let's test whether this model can improve the performance of this regression task:

Code Block 7-16

```python
from river.tree import SGTRegressor
# model pipeline
model = SGTRegressor()
# fit the model
for x_i,y_i in zip(X_train,y_train):
    x_json = {'val'+str(i): x for i,x in enumerate(x_i)}
    model.learn_one(x_json,y_i)
# predict on the test set
preds = []
for x_i in X_test:
    x_json = {'val'+str(i): x for i,x in enumerate(x_i)}
    preds.append(model.predict_one(x_json))
# compute accuracy
r2_score(y_test, preds)
```

2. The result is worse than the previous models, as it is 0.07. Let's again see whether it can be optimized using hyperparameter tuning:

Code Block 7-17

```python
from river.tree import SGTRegressor
def evaluate_SGT(delta, lambda_value, grace_period):
    # model pipeline
    model = SGTRegressor(delta=delta,
                         lambda_value=lambda_value,
                         grace_period=grace_period,)
```

```
    # fit the model
    for x_i,y_i in zip(X_train,y_train):
        x_json = {'val'+str(i): x for i,x in
enumerate(x_i)}
        model.learn_one(x_json,y_i)
    # predict on the test set
    preds = []
    for x_i in X_test:
        x_json = {'val'+str(i): x for i,x in
enumerate(x_i)}
        preds.append(model.predict_one(x_json))
    # compute accuracy
    return r2_score(y_test, preds)
```

3. For this trial, we'll optimize the `grace_period`, `lambda_value`, and `delta` hyperparameters:

Code Block 7-18

```
grace_periods=[0,10,25]
lambda_values=[0.5, 0.8, 1.]
deltas=[0.0001, 0.001, 0.01, 0.1]
```

4. You can run the optimization loop using the following code:

Code Block 7-19

```
results = []
i = 0
for grace_period in grace_periods:
    for lambda_value in lambda_values:
        for delta in deltas:
            print(i)
            i = i+1
            result = evaluate_SGT(delta, lambda_value,
grace_period)
            print(result)
            results.append([delta, lambda_value, grace_
period,result])
```

5. The best results can be shown using the following line of code:

Code Block 7-20

```
pd.DataFrame(results, columns=['delta', 'lambda_value',
'grace_period', 'r2_score' ]).sort_values('r2_score',
ascending=False)
```

The result is shown in the following:

	delta	lambda_value	grace_period	r2_score
14	0.0100	0.5	10	0.317541
15	0.1000	0.5	10	0.307490
23	0.1000	1.0	10	0.303276
26	0.0100	0.5	25	0.298743
27	0.1000	0.5	25	0.291005
18	0.0100	0.8	10	0.285760
19	0.1000	0.8	10	0.282097
12	0.0001	0.5	10	0.273438
31	0.1000	0.8	25	0.272228
34	0.0100	1.0	25	0.266695
30	0.0100	0.8	25	0.257432
16	0.0001	0.8	10	0.250889
13	0.0010	0.5	10	0.247436
35	0.1000	1.0	25	0.246501

Figure 7.7 – The resulting output of Code Block 7-20

The result is better than the non-tuned SGTRegressor, but much worse than the previous two models. The model could be optimized further, but it does not seem the best go-to for the current data.

Regression algorithm 4 – SRPRegressor

SRPRegressor, or **Streaming Random Patches regressor**, is an ensemble method that trains an ensemble of base learners on subsets of the input data. These subsets are called **patches** and are both subsets of features and subsets of observations. This is the same approach as the **random forest** that was seen in the previous chapter.

SRPRegressor in River

We will check this out using the following example:

1. In this example, let's use linear regression as a base learner, as this model has had the best performance compared to the other models tested in this chapter:

Code Block 7-21

```
from river.ensemble import SRPRegressor
# model pipeline
base_model = LinearRegression()
model = SRPRegressor(
    model=base_model,
    n_models=3,
    seed=42
)
# fit the model
for x_i,y_i in zip(X_train,y_train):
    x_json = {'val'+str(i): x for i,x in enumerate(x_i)}
    model.learn_one(x_json,y_i)
# predict on the test set
preds = []
for x_i in X_test:
    x_json = {'val'+str(i): x for i,x in enumerate(x_i)}
    preds.append(model.predict_one(x_json))
# compute accuracy
r2_score(y_test, preds)
```

2. The resulting score is 0.34. Let's try and tune the number of models used to see whether this can improve performance:

Code Block 7-22

```
def evaluate_SRP(n_models):
    # model pipeline
    base_model = LinearRegression()
    model = SRPRegressor(
        model=base_model,
```

```
            n_models=n_models,
            seed=42
    )
    # fit the model
    for x_i,y_i in zip(X_train,y_train):
        x_json = {'val'+str(i): x for i,x in
enumerate(x_i)}
        model.learn_one(x_json,y_i)
    # predict on the test set
    preds = []
    for x_i in X_test:
        x_json = {'val'+str(i): x for i,x in
enumerate(x_i)}
        preds.append(model.predict_one(x_json))
    # compute accuracy
    return r2_score(y_test, preds)
```

3. You can execute the tuning loop with the following code:

Code Block 7-23

```
results = []
for n_models in range(1, 50):
    results.append([n_models, evaluate_SRP(n_models)])
```

4. The following line shows the results for each value of n_models:

Code Block 7-24

```
pd.DataFrame(results,columns=['n_models', 'r2_score']).
sort_values('r2_score', ascending=False)
```

The result is shown in the following:

	n_models	r2_score
12	13	0.457266
29	30	0.437013
44	45	0.433339
10	11	0.432692
32	33	0.430555
25	26	0.424293
38	39	0.423461
30	31	0.422164
20	21	0.421289
24	25	0.421262
13	14	0.417958
18	19	0.414749
9	10	0.414242
14	15	0.412866
42	43	0.410502
40	41	0.410082

Figure 7.8 – The resulting output of Code Block 7-24

Apparently, the result at 12 models has found a sweet spot at which the performance is `0.457`. Compared to the simple `LinearRegression` model with a score of `0.478`, this is a worse result. This indicates that the `LinearRegression` model has the best score of the four models tested in this dataset.

Of course, this result is strongly related to the data-generating process that is behind the `make_regression` function. If the `make_regression` function were to add anything such as time trends, the adaptive models would probably have been more performant than the simple linear model.

Summary

In this chapter, you have seen the basics of regression modeling. You have learned that there are some similarities between classification and anomaly detection models, but that there are also some fundamental differences.

The main difference in regression is that the target variables are numeric, whereas they are categorical in classification. This introduces a difference in metrics, but also in the model definition and the way the models work deep down.

You have seen several traditional, offline regression models and their adaptation to working in an online training manner. You have also seen some online regression models that are made specifically for online training and streaming.

As in the previous chapters, you have seen how to implement a modeling benchmark using a train-test set. The field of ML does not stop evolving, and newer and better models are published regularly. This introduces the need for practitioners to be solid in their skills to evaluate models.

Mastering model evaluation is often even more important than knowing the largest list of models. You need to know a large number of models to start modeling, but it is the evaluation that will allow you to avoid pushing erroneous or overfitted models into production.

Although this is generally true for ML, the next chapter will introduce a category of models that has a fundamentally different take on this. Reinforcement learning is a category of online ML in which the focus is on model updating. Online models have the capacity to learn on each piece of data that gets into the system as well, but reinforcement learning is focused even more on having almost autonomous learning. This will be the scope of the next chapter.

Further reading

- *LinearRegression*: https://riverml.xyz/latest/api/linear-model/LinearRegression/

- *Make_regression*: https://scikit-learn.org/stable/modules/generated/sklearn.datasets.make_regression.html

- *HoeffdingAdaptiveTreeRegressor*: https://riverml.xyz/latest/api/tree/HoeffdingAdaptiveTreeRegressor/

- *HoeffdingAdaptiveTreeClassifier*: https://riverml.xyz/latest/api/tree/HoeffdingAdaptiveTreeClassifier/

- *Adaptive learning and mining for data streams and frequent patterns*: https://dl.acm.org/doi/abs/10.1145/1656274.1656287

- *SGTRegressor*: https://riverml.xyz/latest/api/tree/SGTRegressor/

- *SRPRegressor*: https://riverml.xyz/latest/api/ensemble/SRPRegressor/

8
Reinforcement Learning

The reinforcement learning paradigm is very different than standard machine learning and even the online machine learning methods that we have covered in earlier chapters. Although reinforcement learning will not always be a better choice than "regular" learning for many use cases, it is a powerful tool for tackling re-learning and the adaptation of models.

In reinforcement learning, we give the model a lot of decisive power to do its re-learning and to update the rules of its decision-making process. Rather than letting the model make a prediction and hardcode the action to take for this prediction, the model will directly decide on the action to take.

For automated machine learning pipelines in which actions are effectively automated, this can be a great choice. Of course, this must be complemented with different types of logging, monitoring, and more. For cases in which we need a prediction rather than an action, reinforcement learning will not be appropriate.

Although very powerful in the right use case, reinforcement learning is currently not a standard choice with respect to regular machine learning. In the future, reinforcement learning may very well gain popularity for a larger number of use cases.

In this chapter, you will first be thoroughly introduced to the different concepts behind reinforcement learning. You will then see an implementation of reinforcement learning in Python.

This chapter covers the following topics:

- Defining reinforcement learning
- The main steps of reinforcement learning models
- Exploring Q-learning
- Deep Q-learning
- Using reinforcement learning for streaming data
- Use cases of reinforcement learning
- Implementing reinforcement learning in Python

Technical requirements

You can find all the code for this book on GitHub at the following link: `https://github.com/PacktPublishing/Machine-Learning-for-Streaming-Data-with-Python`. If you are not yet familiar with Git and GitHub, the easiest way to download the notebooks and code samples is the following:

1. Go to the link of the repository.
2. Go to the green **Code** button.
3. Select **Download zip**.

When you download the ZIP file, you unzip it in your local environment, and you will be able to access the code through your preferred Python editor.

Python environment

To follow along with this book, you can download the code in the repository and execute it using your preferred Python editor.

If you are not yet familiar with Python environments, I would advise you to check out either Anaconda (`https://www.anaconda.com/products/individual`), which comes with the Jupyter Notebook and JupyterLab, which are both great for executing notebooks. It also comes with Spyder and VSCode for editing scripts and programs.

If you have difficulty installing Python or the associated programs on your machine, you can check out Google Colab (`https://colab.research.google.com/`) or Kaggle Notebooks (`https://www.kaggle.com/code`), which both allow you to run Python code in online notebooks for free, without any setup.

> **Note**
> The code in the book will generally use Colab and Kaggle notebooks with Python version 3.7.13 and you can set up your own environment to mimic this.

Defining reinforcement learning

Reinforcement learning is a subdomain of machine learning that focuses on creating machine learning models that make decisions. Sometimes, the models are not referred to as models, but rather as intelligent agents.

When looking from a distance, you could argue that reinforcement learning is very close to machine learning. We could say that both of them are methods inside artificial intelligence that try to deliver intelligent black boxes, which are able to learn specific tasks just like a human would – often better.

If we look closer, however, we start to see important differences. In previous chapters, you have seen machine learning models such as anomaly detection, classification, and regression. All of them use a number of variables and are able to make real-time predictions on a target variable based on those.

You have seen a number of metrics that allow us data scientists to decide whether a model is any good. The online models are also able to adapt to changing data by relearning and continuously taking into account their own error metrics.

Reinforcement learning goes further than that. RL models not only make predictions but also take action. You could say that offline models do not take any autonomy in relearning from their mistakes, online models do take into account mistakes right away, and reinforcement learning models are designed to make mistakes and learn from them.

Online models can adapt to their mistakes, just like reinforcement learning. However, when you build the first version of an online model, you do expect it to have acceptable performance in the beginning, and you would train it on some historical data. It can then adapt in the case of data drift or other changes.

The reinforcement learning model, on the other hand, starts out totally naïve and unknowing. It will try out actions, make some mistakes, and then by pure hazard at some point, it will make some good decisions as well. At this point, the reinforcement model will receive rewards and start to remember those.

Comparing online and offline reinforcement learning

Reinforcement learning is generally online learning: the intelligent agent learns through repeated action taking with rewards for good predictions. This can continue indefinitely, at least as long as feedback on the decision keeps getting fed into the model.

However, reinforcement learning can also be offline. In this case, the model would learn for a given period of time, and then at some point, the feedback loop is cut off so that the model (the decision rules) stays the same after that point.

In general, when reinforcement learning is used, it is because we are interested in continuous relearning. So, the online variant is the most common.

A more detailed overview of feedback loops in reinforcement learning

Now, let's go more into the details of reinforcement learning. To start, it is important to understand how the feedback loop of a general reinforcement learning model works. The following schema shows the logic of a model learning through a feedback loop.

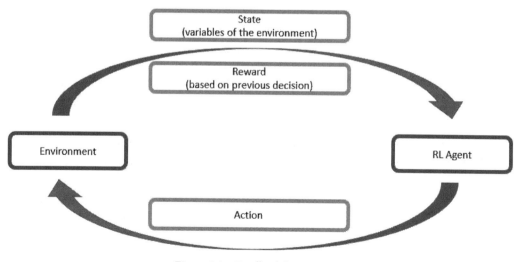

Figure 8.1 – Feedback loops in RL

In this schema, you observe the following elements:

- **The RL agent**: Our model that is continuously learning and making decisions.
- **The environment**: A fixed environment in which the agent can make a specific set of decisions.
- **The action**: Every time the agent makes a decision, this will alter the environment.
- **The reward**: If the decision yields a good result, then a reward will be given to the agent.
- **The state**: The information about the environment that the agent needs to make its decisions.

As a simplified example, imagine that the agent is a human baby learning to walk. At each point in time, the baby is trying out stuff that could get them to walk. More specifically, they are activating several muscles in their body.

While doing this, the baby is observing that they are or are not walking. Also, their parents cheer them on when they are getting closer to walking correctly. This is a reward being sent to the baby that indicates to them that they are learning in the right way.

The baby will then again try to walk by using almost the same muscles, but with a little variation. If it's better, they'll see that as a positive thing and continue to move in that way.

Let's now cover the remaining steps that are necessary for all of this to work.

The main steps of a reinforcement learning model

The actions of the agent are the decisions that it can make. This is a limited set of decisions. As you will understand, the agent is just a piece of code, so all its decisions will need to be programmed controls of its own behavior.

If we think of it as a computer game, then you understand that the actions that you as a player can execute are limited by the buttons that you can press on your game console. All of the combinations together still allow for a very wide range of options, but they are limited in some way.

The same is true for our human baby learning to walk. They only have control over their own body, so they would not be able to execute any actions beyond this. This gives a huge number of things that can be done by humans, but still, it is a fixed set of actions.

Making the decisions

Now, as your reinforcement agent is receiving information about its environment (the state), it will need to convert this information into a decision. This is the same idea as a machine learning model that needs to map independent variables into a target variable.

This decision mapping is generally called the policy in the case of reinforcement learning. The policy will generally decide on the best action by estimating the expected rewards and then executing the action with the highest expected reward.

Updating the decision rules

The last part of this big picture description of reinforcement learning is the update of the policy: basically, the learning itself. There are many models, and they all have their own specificities, but let's try to get a general idea anyway.

At this point, you have seen that an agent takes an action from a set of fixed actions. The agent has estimated which is most likely to maximize rewards. After the execution of this task, the model will receive a certain reward. This will be used to alter the policy, in a way that depends on the exact method of reinforcement learning that you use.

In the next section, you will see how this can be done in more detail by exploring the Q-learning algorithm.

Exploring Q-learning

Although there are many variants of reinforcement learning, the previous explanation should have given you a good general overview of how most reinforcement models work. It is now time to move deeper into a specific model for reinforcement learning: Q-learning.

Q-learning is a reinforcement learning algorithm that is, so-called, model free. Model-free reinforcement learning algorithms can be seen as pure trial-and-error algorithms: they have no prior notion of the environment, but merely just try out actions and learn whether their actions yield the correct outcome.

Model-based algorithms, on the other hand, use a different theoretical approach. Rather than just learning the outcome based on the actions, they try to understand their environment through some form of a model. Once the agent learns how the environment works, it can take actions that will optimize the reward according to this knowledge.

Although the model-based approach may seem more intuitively likely to perform, model-free approaches such as Q-learning are actually quite good.

The goal of Q-learning

The goal of the Q-learning algorithm is to find a policy that maximizes the expected reward obtained from a number of successive steps starting at the current state.

In regular language, this means that Q-learning looks at the current state (the variables of its environment) and then uses this information to take the best steps in the future. The model does not look at past happenings, only the future.

The model uses the Q-value as a calculation for the quality of a state-action combination: that is, for each state, there is a list of potential actions. Each combination of a potential state and a potential action is called a state-action combination. The Q-value indicates the quality of this action when the state is the given one.

At the beginning of the reinforcement learning process, the value of Q is initialized in some way (randomly or fixed) and then updates every time that a reward is received. The agent handles the model according to the Q-values, and when rewards (feedback on the actions) start to come in, those Q values change. The agent still continues to follow the Q-values, but as they update, the behavior of the agent changes.

The core of this algorithm is the Bellman equation: an update rule for Q-values that uses a weighted average of older and new Q-values. Therefore, old information is forgotten at some point, when a lot of learning has happened. This avoids getting "stuck" in previous behaviors.

The formula of the Bellman equation is the following:

$$Q_{new}(s_t, a_t) = Q(s_t, a_t) + \alpha * (r_t + \gamma * \max Q(s_{t+1}, a) - Q(s_t, a_t))$$

Parameters of the Q-learning algorithm

In this Bellman equation, there are a few important parameters that you can tune. Let's briefly cover those:

- The learning rate is a very commonly used hyperparameter in machine learning algorithms. It generally defines the step size of an optimizer in which large steps may make you move around faster in the optimization space, but too large steps may also cause a problem to go into narrow optimums.

- The discount factor is a concept that is very often used in finance and economics. In reinforcement learning, it indicates at which rate the model needs to prioritize short-term or long-term rewards.

After this overview of Q-learning, the next section will introduce a more complex alternative version of this approach called Deep Q-learning.

Deep Q-learning

Now that you have seen the basics of reinforcement learning and the most basic reinforcement learning model, Q-learning, it is time to move on to a more performant and more commonly used model called Deep Q-learning.

Deep Q-learning is a variant of Q-learning in which the Q-values are not just a list of expected Q-values for each combination of state and actions, updated by the Bellman equation. Rather, in Deep Q-learning, this estimation is done using a (deep) neural network.

If you are not familiar, neural networks are a class of machine learning models that are amongst the state of the art in terms of performance. Neural networks are largely used for many use cases in artificial intelligence, machine learning, and data science in general. Deep neural networks are the technology that allows many data science use cases such as **Natural Language Processing (NLP)**, computer vision, and much more.

The idea behind the neural network is to pass an input data point through a network of nodes, called neurons, that each do a very simple operation. The fact that there are many such simple operations being done, and weights applied in between, means that the neural network is a powerful learning algorithm for mapping input data into a target variable.

The following example shows a standard depiction of a neural network. The models can be as simple or as complex as you want. You can go to huge numbers of hidden layers and add as many nodes per hidden layer as you want. Each arrow is a coefficient and needs to be estimated. So, it must be kept in mind that a large quantity of data will be necessary for estimating such models.

The example schematic of a neural network is shown here:

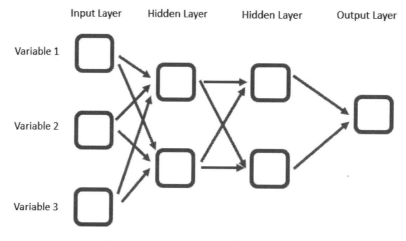

Figure 8.2 – Neural network architecture

For reinforcement learning, this has to be applied inside the Q-learning paradigm. In essence, the deep learning model is just a better way to estimate Q-values than the standard Q-learning approach (or at least that's what it aspires to be).

You could see the analogy as follows. In standard Q-learning, there is a relatively simple storage and update mechanism for new rewards coming in and updating the policy. You could see it as depicted as a table, as follows:

State	Action	Q-value
1	A	....
1	B	....
1	C	....
2	A	....
2	B	....
2	C	....
...	...	....

Figure 8.3 – Example table format

In Deep Q-learning, the input and output processes are mostly the same, yet the state is transcribed as a number of variables that are input into a neural network. The neural network then outputs the estimated Q-values for each action.

The following graph shows how the state is added as input to the neural network.

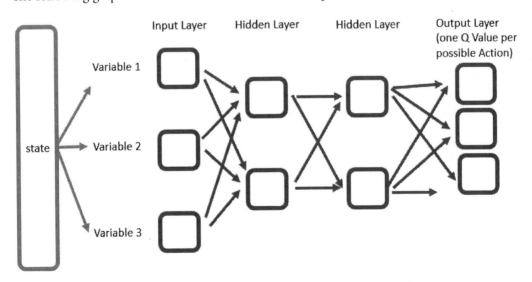

Figure 8.4 – Adding the state as input to the neural network

Now that you understand the theory behind reinforcement learning, the next section will be more applied as it presents a number of example use cases for reinforcement learning on streaming data.

Using reinforcement learning for streaming data

As discussed throughout earlier chapters, the challenge of building models on streaming data is to find models that are able to learn incrementally and that are able to adapt in the case of model drift or data drift.

Reinforcement learning is a potential candidate that could respond well to those two challenges. After all, reinforcement learning has a feedback loop that allows it to change policy when many mistakes are made. It is therefore able to adapt itself in the event of changes.

Reinforcement learning can be seen as a subcase of online learning. At the same time, the second specificity of reinforcement learning is its focus on learning actions, whereas regular online models are focused on making accurate predictions.

The split between the two fields is present in practice in the types of use cases and domains of application, but many streaming use cases have the potential to benefit from reinforcement learning and it is a great toolset to master.

If you are looking for more depth and examples, you can look at the following insightful article: `https://www.researchgate.net/publication/337581742_ Machine_learning_for_streaming_data_state_of_the_art_ challenges_and_opportunities`.

In the next section, we will explore a few key use cases where reinforcement learning proves crucial.

Use cases of reinforcement learning

The use cases of reinforcement learning are almost as numerous as online learning. It is a less often used technology when compared to standard offline and online models, but with the changes in the machine learning domain over the last years, it is still a great candidate that could become huge in the coming years.

Let's look at some use cases to get a better feel of the types of use cases that can be suitable for reinforcement learning. Among the types of examples, there are some that are more traditional reinforcement learning use cases, and others that are more specific streaming data use cases.

Use case one – trading system

As a first use case of reinforcement learning, let's talk about stock market trading. The stock market use case was already discussed in the forecasting use case of the regression chapter. Reinforcement learning is an alternative solution to it.

In regression, online models are used to build forecasting tools. Using these forecasting tools, a stock trader could predict the price developments of specific stocks in the near future and use those predictions to decide on buying or selling the stocks.

Using reinforcement learning, the use case would be developed slightly differently. The intelligent agent would learn how to make decisions rather than to predict prices. As an example, you could give the agent three actions: sell, buy, or hold (hold meaning do nothing/ignore).

The agent would receive information about its environment, which could include past stock prices, macroeconomic information, and much more. This information would be used together with a policy and this policy decides when to buy, sell, or hold.

By training this agent for a long period of time, and with a lot of data including all types of market scenarios, the agent could learn pretty well how to trade markets. You would then obtain a profitable "trading robot," making money without much intervention. If successful, this is clearly an advantage over regression models as they only predict price and do not take any action.

For more information on this topic, you could start by checking out the following links:

- `https://arxiv.org/pdf/1911.10107.pdf`
- `http://cslt.riit.tsinghua.edu.cn/mediawiki/images/a/`
  `aa/07407387.pdf`

Use case two – social network ranking system

A second use case for reinforcement learning is the ranking of posts on social networks. The general idea of what happens behind this is a number of posts being created and the most relevant has to be shown to each specific user, based on their preference.

There are many machine learning approaches that could be leveraged for this, and reinforcement learning is one of them. Basically, the model would end up making decisions on the posts to show to the user, so in this way, it is a real action that is taken.

This action also generates feedback. If the user likes, comments, shares, clicks, pauses, or interacts in other ways with the post, the agent will be rewarded and learns that this type of post does interest the user.

By trial and error, the agent can publish different types of posts to each user and learn which decisions are good and which are bad.

Real-time response is very important here, as well as learning rapidly from mistakes. If a user receives a number of irrelevant posts, this would be detrimental to their user experience and the model should learn as soon as possible that its predictions are not correct. Online learning or reinforcement learning is therefore great for this use case.

For more information about such use cases, you can find some materials here:

- `https://arxiv.org/abs/1601.00667`
- `https://rbcdsai.iitm.ac.in/blogs/finding-influencers-in-social-networks-reinforcement-learning-shows-the-way/`

Use case three – a self-driving car

Reinforcement learning has also been proposed for the use case of self-driving cars. As you probably know, self-driving cars have been increasingly gaining attention over the last few years. The goal is to make machine learning or artificial intelligence models that can replace the behavior of human drivers.

It is easy to understand that the essential part of this model will be to take actions: accelerate, slow down, brake, turn, and so on. If a good enough reinforcement learning model could be built to obtain all those skills, it would be a great candidate for building self-driving cars.

Self-driving cars need to respond to a large stream of data about the environment. For example, they need to detect cars, roads, road signs, and much more on a continuous video stream that is being filmed on multiple cameras, together with other sensors potentially.

Real-time responses are key in this scenario. Retraining the model in real time might be more problematic, as you would want to make sure that the model is not applying a trial-and-error methodology while on the road.

More information on this can be found at the following links:

- `https://arxiv.org/ftp/arxiv/papers/1901/1901.00569.pdf`
- `https://www.ingentaconnect.com/contentone/ist/ei/2017/00002017/00000019/art00012?crawler=true&mimetype=application/pdf`

Use case four – chatbots

Another very different but also very advanced use case of machine learning is the development of chatbots. Intelligent chatbots are still rare, but we can expect to see chatbots become more intelligent in the near future.

Chatbots need to be able to generate a response to a person while treating the information that was given to it by a user. The chatbot is therefore performing a sort of action: replying to the human.

Reinforcement learning in combination with other techniques from the domain of natural language processing can be a good solution for such problems. By letting the chatbot talk with users, a reward can be given by the human user in the form of, for example, an evaluation of the usefulness of their interaction. This reward can then help the reinforcement learning agent adapt its policy and make replies more appropriate in future interactions.

Chatbots need to be able to respond in real time, as no one wants to wait for an answer from a chatbot interaction. Learning can be done in an online or an offline fashion, but reinforcement learning is definitely one of the suitable alternatives.

You can read more on this use case here:

- `https://arxiv.org/abs/1709.02349`
- `https://arxiv.org/pdf/1908.10331.pdf`

Use case five – learning games

As a final use case example for reinforcement learning, let's talk about the use case of learning games. It may be less valuable for business, but it is still an interesting use case of reinforcement learning.

Over the past years, reinforcement learning agents have learned to play a number of games, including chess and Go. There is a clear set of moves that can be made at each step, and by playing many simulated (or real) games, the models can learn which policy (decision rules for the step to take) are the best.

In the end, the agent has such a powerful policy that it can often beat the best human players in the world at such games.

You can find more examples of this at the following links:

- `https://www.science.org/doi/10.1126/science.aar6404`
- `https://arxiv.org/pdf/1912.10944.pdf`

Now that we have explored some of the use cases for reinforcement learning, let's implement it using Python, in the next section.

Implementing reinforcement learning in Python

Let's now move on to an example in which streaming data is used for Q-Learning. The data that we will be using is simulated data of stock prices:

1. The data is generated in the following block of code.

   The list of values that is first generated is a list of 30,000 consecutive values that represent stock prices. The data generating process is the starting point of 0 and at every time step, there is a random value added to this. The random normal values are centered around 0, which indicates that prices would go up or down by a step size based on a standard deviation of 1.

This process is often referred to as a random walk and it can go quite far up or down. After that, the values are standardized to be within a normal distribution again.

Code Block 8-1

```python
import numpy as np
import matplotlib.pyplot as plt
import random


starting = 0
values = [starting]
for i in range(30000):
    values.append(values[-1] + np.random.normal())


values = (values - np.mean(values)) / np.std(values)
plt.plot(values)
```

The resulting plot can be seen in the following:

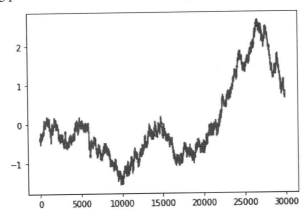

Figure 8.5 – The resulting plot from the preceding code block

2. Now, for a reinforcement problem, it is necessary to have a finite number of states. Of course, if we consider stock prices, we could collect up to an infinite number of decimals. The data is rounded to 1 decimal to limit the number of possible state data points:

Code Block 8-2

```
rounded_values = []
for value in values:
    rounded_values.append(round(value, 1))


plt.plot(rounded_values)
```

The resulting graph is shown in the following figure:

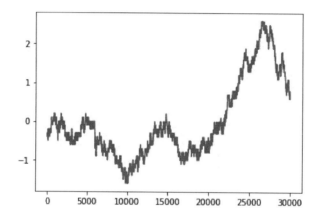

Figure 8.6 – The graph resulting from the preceding code block

3. We can now set the states' potential values to all of the values that have happened in the past. We can also initiate a policy.

As seen in the theoretical part of this chapter, the policy represents the rules of the reinforcement learning agent. In some cases, there is a very specific ruleset, but in Q-learning, there is only a Q-value (quality) for each combination of state and action.

In our example, let's consider a stock trading bot that can only do two things at a time *t*. Either the trading bot buys at time *t* and sells at *t+1*, or it sells at time *t* and closes the sell position at time *t+1*. Without going into stock trading too much, the important things to understand about this are the following:

- When the agent buys, it should do so because it expects the stock market to go up.

- When the agent opens a sell order, it should do so because it expects the stock market to go down.

As information, our stock trader will be very limited. The only data point in the state is the price at time t. The goal here is not to make a great model, but to show the principles of building a reinforcement learning agent on a stock trading example. In reality, you'd need much more information in the state to decide on your action:

Code Block 8-3

```
states = set(rounded_values)
import pandas as pd
policy = pd.DataFrame(0, index=states, columns=['buy',
'sell'])
```

4. The function defined hereafter is how to obtain an action (sell or buy) based on the Q-table. It is not entirely correct to refer to the Q table as the policy, but it does make it more understandable.

The action chosen is that with the highest Q value for a given state (state is the current value of the stock):

Code Block 8-4

```
def find_action(policy, current_value):

    if policy.loc[current_value,:].sum() == 0:
        return random.choice([ 'buy', 'sell'])


    return policy.columns[policy.loc[current_value,:].
argmax()]
```

5. It is also necessary to define an update rule. In this example, the update rule is based on the Bellman equation that was explained earlier on. However, keep in mind that the agent is fairly simple, and the discounting part is not really relevant. Discounting is useful to make an agent prefer short-term gains over long-term gains. The current agent always makes its gains in one time step, so discounting is of no added value. In a real stock-trading bot, this would be very important: you wouldn't put your money on a stock that will double over 20 years if you could double it in 1 year instead:

Code Block 8-5

```
def update_policy(reward, current_state_value, action):

    LEARNING_RATE = 0.1
    MAX_REWARD = 10
    DISCOUNT_FACTOR = 0.05


    return LEARNING_RATE * (reward + DISCOUNT_FACTOR *
MAX_REWARD - policy.loc[current_state_value,action])
```

6. We now get to the execution of the model. We start by setting past_state to 0 and past_action to buy. The total reward is initialized at 0 and an accumulator list for rewards is instantiated.

    The code will then loop through the rounded values. This is a process that copies a data stream. If the data arrived one by one, the agent would be able to learn in exactly the same manner. The essence is an update of the Q table at every learning step.

    Within each iteration, the model will execute the best action, where the best is based on the Q values of the Q values table (policy). The model will also receive the reward from time step t-1, as this was defined as the only option for the stock trading bot. Those rewards will be used to update the Q table so that the next round can have updated information:

Code Block 8-6

```
past_state_value = 0
past_action = 'buy'
total_reward = 0.
rewards = []
```

```
for i, current_state_value in enumerate(rounded_values):

    # do the action
    action = find_action(policy, current_state_value)


    # also compute reward from previous action and update
state
    if past_action == 'buy':
        reward = current_state_value - past_state_value

    if past_action == 'sell':
        reward = past_state_value - current_state_value

    total_reward = total_reward + float(reward)

    policy.loc[current_state_value, action] = policy.
loc[current_state_value, action] + update_policy(reward,
current_state_value,action)

    #print(policy)
    rewards.append(total_reward)

    past_action = action
    past_state_value = current_state_value
```

7. In the following plot, you see how the model is getting its rewards. In the beginning, total rewards are negative for a long time, and then they are positive at the end. Keep in mind that we are learning on input data that is hypothetical and that represents a random walk. If we wanted an actual intelligent stock trading bot, we'd need to give it much more and much better data:

Code Block 8-7

```
plt.plot(rewards)
```

The resulting graph is shown hereafter:

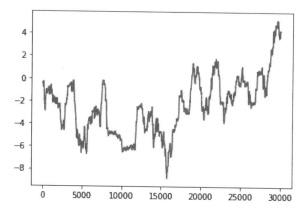

Figure 8.7 – The graph resulting from the preceding code block

8. The following plot shows a heat map of the Q values against the policy. The values at the top of the table are the preferred action when stock prices are low, and the values at the bottom are preferred actions when stock prices are high. The color light yellow means high-quality actions, and the color black means low-quality actions:

Code Block 8-8

```
import seaborn as sns
sns.heatmap(policy.sort_index())
```

The resulting heatmap is shown here:

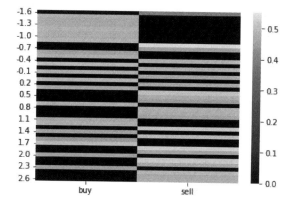

Figure 8.8 – The heatmap resulting from the preceding code block

It is interesting to see that the model seems to have started to learn a basic rule in stock trading: buy low, sell high. This can be seen by more yellow in selling at high prices and more yellow in buying at low prices. Apparently, this rule is even true on simulated random walk data.

To learn more advanced rules, the agent would need to have more data in the state, and therefore the Q table would also become much heavier. An example of what you could add is a rolling history of prices so that the agent knows whether you are in an uptrend or a downtrend. You could also add macro-economic factors, sentiment estimations, or any other data.

You could also make the action structure much more advanced. Rather than having only one-day sell or buy trades, it would be much more interesting to have a model that can buy or sell any equity in its portfolio at any time that the agent decides to.

Of course, you would also need to provide enough data to allow the model to make estimations for all these scenarios. The more scenarios you take into account, the more time it will take the agent to learn how to behave correctly.

Summary

In this chapter, you were first introduced to the underlying foundations of reinforcement learning. You saw that reinforcement learning models are focused on taking actions rather than on making predictions.

You also saw two widely known algorithms for reinforcement learning. This started with Q-learning, which is the foundational algorithm of reinforcement learning, and its more powerful improvement, Deep Q-learning.

Reinforcement learning is often used for more advanced use cases such as chatbots or self-driving cars, but can also be used for numerical data streams very well. Through a use case, you saw how to apply reinforcement learning to streaming data for finance.

With this chapter, you have come to the end of discovering the most relevant machine learning models for online learning. In the coming chapters, you will discover a number of additional tools that you will need to take into account in online learning and that have no real counterpart in traditional ML. You will first have a deep dive into all types of data and model drift and then discover how to deal with models that go totally in the wrong direction through catastrophic forgetting.

Further reading

- Reinforcement learning applications: `https://neptune.ai/blog/reinforcement-learning-applications`

- Q-learning: `https://en.wikipedia.org/wiki/Q-learning`

- Deep Q-learning: `https://en.wikipedia.org/wiki/Deep_reinforcement_learning`

Part 3: Advanced Concepts and Best Practices around Streaming Data

This part will cover some of the advanced topics around streaming data, including drift and feature transformation. We will use examples to learn about each of these concepts. Finally, we will wrap up everything we learned in the last chapter, as a summary of all the topics.

This section comprises the following chapters:

- *Chapter 9, Drift and Drift Detection*
- *Chapter 10, Feature Transformation and Scaling*
- *Chapter 11, Catastrophic Forgetting*
- *Chapter 12, Conclusion and Best Practices*

9
Drift and Drift Detection

Throughout the previous chapters, you have discovered plenty of ways to build **machine learning** (**ML**) models that work in an online manner. They are able to update their learned decision rules from one single observation rather than having to retrain completely as is common in most ML models.

One reason that this is great is streaming, as these models will allow you to work and learn continuously. However, we could argue that a traditional ML model can also predict on a single observation. Even batch learning and offline models can predict a single new observation at a time. To get more insight into the added value of online ML, this chapter will go in depth into drift and drift detection.

To get to an improved understanding of those concepts, the chapter will start with an in-depth description of what drift is. You will then see different types of drift, including concept drift, data drift, and retraining strategy issues.

After that, you will be exposed to a number of methods to detect both data drift and concept drift. You will also see a number of methods to counteract drift and will be introduced to model explicability and retraining strategies.

For now, let's get started with the basics by having a deeper look at a definition of drift.

This chapter will cover the following topics:

- Defining drift
- Introducing model explicability
- Measuring drift
- Measuring drift in Python
- Counteracting drift

Technical requirements

You can find all the code for this book on GitHub at the following link: `https://github.com/PacktPublishing/Machine-Learning-for-Streaming-Data-with-Python`. If you are not yet familiar with Git and GitHub, the easiest way to download the notebooks and code samples is by doing the following:

1. Go to the link of the repository.
2. Go to the green **Code** button.
3. Select **Download zip**.

When you download the ZIP file, you unzip it in your local environment, and you will be able to access the code through your preferred Python editor.

Python environment

To follow along with this book, you can download the code in the repository and execute it using your preferred Python editor.

If you are not yet familiar with Python environments, I would advise you to check out Anaconda (`https://www.anaconda.com/products/individual`), which comes with Jupyter Notebook and JupyterLab, which are both great for executing notebooks. It also comes with Spyder and **Visual Studio Code** (**VS Code**) for editing scripts and programs.

If you have difficulty installing Python or the associated programs on your machine, you can check out **Google Colabatory** (**Google Colab**) (`https://colab.research.google.com/`) or Kaggle Notebooks (`https://www.kaggle.com/code`), which both allow you to run Python code in online notebooks for free, without any setup required.

> **Note**
> The code in the book will generally use Colab and Kaggle Notebooks with Python version 3.7.13, and you can set up your own environment to mimic this.

Defining drift

It is a well-known and commonly observed problem that models tend to start performing worse with time. Whether your metric is accuracy, R2 score, F1 score, or anything else, you will see a slow but steady decrease in performance over time if you put models into production and do not update them.

Depending on your use case, this decrease may become problematic quickly or slowly. Some use cases need to have continuous, near-perfect predictions. In some use cases— for example, for specialized ML in which the models have a direct impact on life—you would be strongly shocked if you observed a 1 percent decrease. In other use cases, ML is used more as automation than as prediction, and the business partners may not even notice a 5 percent decrease.

Whether it is going to impact you is not the question here. What is sure, is that in general, you will see your models decreasing. The goal for this chapter is to make sure to find out why model performance is decreasing, how you can measure it, and what can be done about it if you decide that it is too problematic for your use case.

In the next section, we will start by presenting three different types of drift that you may encounter in streaming use cases.

Three types of drift

There are two reasons for drift that are generally considered with streaming data: concept drift and data drift. In this part, you will first discover concept and data drift, but you will also see how retraining strategies can have an impact on your model drifting away from the data rather than the opposite.

Concept drift

In concept drift, we try to explain worsening model performance by a change in the concept that we are modeling. This means that the statistical properties of the target variable are changing, and therefore the model is no longer adequate for our use case.

A simplified example of concept change is a model that tries to forecast hot chocolate sales of a certain bar. Maybe the model was perfect for a certain while, but at some point, a competing bar got installed in the area. The underlying demand process has changed, and this was logically not included in the model, as the competition was not relevant when the model was built.

When the concept changes, the model needs to be updated to take into account the most recent processes, as the model is no longer adequate for the use case. The following schematic diagram shows what goes wrong in the case of concept drift:

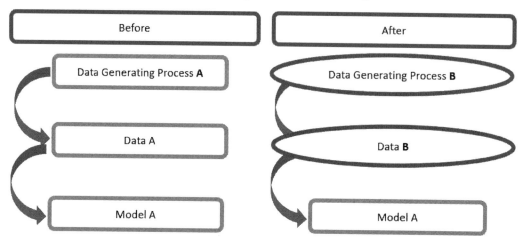

Figure 9.1 – Concept drift

Now that you have seen the theory behind concept drift, the next section will present data drift—a second important type of drift.

Data drift

When we talk about data drift, we talk about a change in the statistical properties of independent variables. This is mainly relevant when we have worked with a sample of data (maybe just based on what we had available), but then we start to realize that the sample is no longer representative of the data that we are receiving at the current moment.

Examples include changes in measurement machines, where a new measurement device may give slightly different measurements than the old material. Imagine we change the thermometer and our new thermometer measures about 0.5 degrees higher than the old one. You can understand that the model is not able to take this type of information into account and will make wrong predictions as the model takes the temperature higher than it should.

The following schematic diagram shows what goes wrong in the case of data drift:

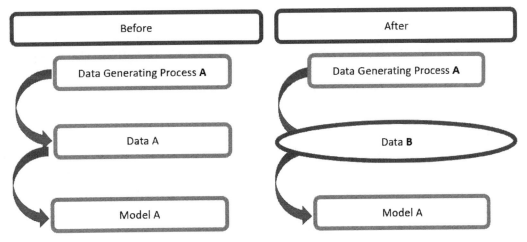

Figure 9.2 – Data drift

Having covered two important causes of drift, the next section will present model decay and misspecification—a third drift-related problem.

Model decay and misspecification

Although not generally considered a problem of drift in the literature, I find it important to also mention problems with the model as one of the problems behind drifting and decaying performance. In real-life situations, humans are imperfect and make mistakes. Theoretically, we should expect models to be well specified and therefore not be the reasons for any problems.

In practice, however, retraining of models may be wrongly automated, thereby introducing small problems that slowly, with time, add up to large problems, and this may be an important reason for model decay and lowering performance.

The following schematic diagram shows what goes wrong in the case of model problems, due to any reason such as misspecification or retraining problems:

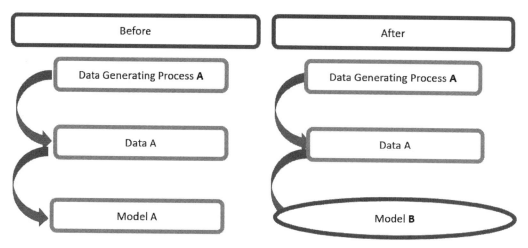

Figure 9.3 – Model-induced problems

Having seen three potential reasons for drift in streaming models, the next section will explain how model explicability can be used as a solution against drift.

Introducing model explicability

When models are learning in an online fashion, they are repeatedly relearning. This relearning process is happening automatically, and it is often impossible for a human user to keep an eye on the models continuously. In addition, this would go against the main goal of doing ML as the goal is to let machines—or models—take over, rather than having continuous human intervention.

When models learn or relearn, data scientists are generally faced with programmatic model-building interfaces. Imagine a random forest, in which hundreds of decision trees are acting at the same time to predict a target variable for a new observation. Even the task of printing out and looking at all those decisions would be a huge task.

Model explicability is a big topic in recent advances in ML. By throwing black-box models at data-science use cases, big mistakes are occurring. An example is that when self-driving cars were trained on a biased sample containing too many white people, the cars were measured to have more accidents with black people, just because of a data-science error. Understanding what happens in your model can have a life-saving impact.

When considering drift in models, it is also important to understand what happens in your model. The first model that you deploy is likely to be quite close to your expectation. After that, the model will relearn from every data point it encounters. If there are biases in the data, or if biases are occurring from over- or underfitting (and this happens when the model is running in autonomy), then at some point, you are likely to miss out on those trends.

You need to make sure to set up an initial method for model explicability as well as continue to investigate the topic. In the current chapter, we'll be focusing on data drift and concept drift, but keep in mind that model misspecification can also be a huge contributor to decreasing accuracy. This will be covered in more depth in *Chapter 11*.

For now, let's move on to some methods for measuring drift.

Measuring drift

There are two important things to consider for drift. We should first be able to measure drift, as we cannot counteract something that we are not aware of. Secondly, once we become aware of drift, we should define the right strategies for counteracting it. Let's discuss measurements for drift first.

Measuring data drift

As described earlier, data drift means that the measurements are slowly changing over time, whereas the underlying concepts stay the same. To measure this, descriptive statistics can be very useful. As you have seen a lot of descriptive statistics in earlier chapters, we will not repeat the theory behind this.

To apply descriptive statistics to measure data drift, we could simply set up a number of descriptive statistics and track them over time. For each variable, you could set up the following:

- Measurements of centrality (mean, median, mode)
- Measurements of variation (standard deviation, variance, **interquartile range**, or **IQR**)
- Event correlation between the variables

Besides this, it would be necessary to track drift on specific time scales. If you expect drift on very long periods, you could compute these descriptive statistics on a monthly or even yearly basis, but for quicker detection, it could be weekly, daily, or even hourly or more frequent.

The comparison of these metrics over time would allow you to detect a change in the data, which would be a common cause for drift in your model.

Measuring concept drift

When measuring concept drift, the best thing to do is to set up a thorough tracking of model performance over time. The performance metric that you use will depend on your use case and on the type of model you use but may include an R2 score for regression, accuracy, an F1 score for validation, or even more.

When measuring model performance over time, you are likely to see a decrease if no model updating is done. With online models that relearn on every data point, this should theoretically be less of an issue. When you do see your performance decrease, this indicates that something is off somewhere in your system.

If you are already measuring data drift, this would be a good first thing to look at, as data drift is likely to cause decreasing model performance. If data drift is not occurring, you are likely to have a concept drift in your system.

It is important to keep in mind that measuring model drift and data drift are closely linked together in practice: it is hard to attribute decreasing performance to one specific root cause. The goal should be to keep your model performance high and find solutions for this if things are off. Measuring both performance and individual statistics and even more metrics together is what will make your strategy powerful against drift.

Let's now see some Python examples of how to detect drift in modeling.

Measuring drift in Python

When measuring drift, the first thing to do is to make sure that your model is writing out logs or results in some way. For the following example, you'll use a dataset in which each prediction was logged so that we have for each prediction the input variables, the prediction, the ground truth, and the absolute differences between prediction and ground truth as an indicator of error.

Logging your model's behavior is an absolute prerequisite if you want to work on drift detection. Let's start with some basic measurements that could help you to detect drift using Python.

A basic intuitive approach to measuring drift

In this section, you will discover an intuitive approach to measuring drift. Here are the steps we'll follow:

1. To get started measuring drift on our logged results data, we start by importing the data as a pandas DataFrame. This is done in the following code block:

Code block 9-1

```
import pandas as pd
data = pd.read_excel('chapter9datafile.xlsx')
data
```

You will obtain a table that looks like the one shown here:

	Day	X1	X2	X3	Ground Truth	Pred	Error
0	1	0.250298	0.181751	0.181751	0.542658	0.560833	0.018175
1	1	0.443366	0.134283	0.195179	0.044917	0.064435	0.019518
2	1	0.927594	0.272073	0.222386	0.345335	0.367574	0.022239
3	1	0.717674	0.589712	0.281357	0.177930	0.206066	0.028136
4	1	0.373276	0.481404	0.329498	0.537820	0.570769	0.032950
5	1	0.406182	0.250411	0.354539	0.220827	0.256281	0.035454
6	1	0.957131	0.311508	0.385690	0.574584	0.613153	0.038569
7	1	0.560241	0.903281	0.476018	0.497719	0.545321	0.047602
8	1	0.737592	0.646502	0.540668	0.021963	0.076030	0.054067
9	2	0.264116	0.971091	0.637777	0.361884	0.425661	0.063778
10	2	0.432601	0.476053	0.685382	0.512186	0.580724	0.068538
11	2	0.283556	0.764408	0.761823	0.050435	0.126617	0.076182
12	2	0.982049	0.939110	0.855734	0.359503	0.445076	0.085573
13	2	0.145519	0.010305	0.856765	0.670216	0.755893	0.085676
14	2	0.001231	0.994801	0.956245	0.007537	0.103162	0.095624

Figure 9.4 – The data

2. Now that you have the drift-detection data, let's have a look at the development of the error over time by doing a `groupby` operation on the day and looking at the average error, as follows:

Code Block 9-2

```
data.groupby('Day')['Error'].mean()
```

You will obtain the following result:

```
Day
1     0.032968
2     0.089594
3     0.150891
4     0.211815
5     0.267701
Name: Error, dtype: float64
```

Figure 9.5 – The result

You can clearly see that the error is strongly increasing over time, so we can be quite certain that we have a problem with model drift here. Now, of course, it is not yet defined whether this problem is caused by a problem in the data or a problem in the concept.

3. Let's do an analysis with the target variable to see whether the target has experienced large changes over time. The following code does an average of the ground-truth value per day, to see whether there was a clear drift in the target variable:

Code block 9-3

```
data.groupby('Day')['Ground Truth'].mean()
```

The result looks like this:

```
Day
1     0.329306
2     0.395137
3     0.500355
4     0.684496
5     0.554851
Name: Ground Truth, dtype: float64
```

Figure 9.6 – The result (continued)

We do see a quite important change on average over this period.

4. Let's take our inspection further and also do this analysis for each of the independent variables. The following code does an average of the three independent variables per day to see if there is any obvious shift in there:

Code block 9-4

```
data.groupby('Day')[['X1', 'X2', 'X3']].mean()
```

You will obtain the following result:

Day	X1	X2	X3
1	0.597039	0.418992	0.329676
2	0.424838	0.687384	0.895936
3	0.513968	0.567224	1.508915
4	0.468470	0.568075	2.118150
5	0.641704	0.624596	2.677008

Figure 9.7 – The groupby result

We see a very clear change happening in the third explanatory variable, X3. It is highly probable that this is the cause of our model shift.

Measuring drift with robust tools

If you are working on small use cases and you do not want to integrate with large external platforms, the previous examples are really good. However, if you are working at a company where you are limited in resources, it may not be possible or not worth it to develop code for common use cases from scratch.

Drift detection is a use case that is getting quite some popularity at the moment, so more and more robust solutions are being presented to the public—be it paid programs, cloud programs, or open source solutions.

Next, I will present a number of useful solutions that you could look at if you are interested in taking on external platforms for doing your model performance follow-ups and your drift-detection use cases. As those platforms are owned by companies and are sometimes paid, I do not want to go into much depth here, but it is good to give you some pointers in case this is of interest to you.

Soda SQL

One solution that is interesting to look at is Soda SQL. This is a tool that is specific for data quality, so it is not necessarily tuned for ML use cases. However, data quality issues will almost necessarily result in problematic models, so I find it valuable to discuss this solution.

You can find full information here: `https://docs.soda.io/`. Soda SQL is a tool that is really oriented toward data engineering, so I won't go too much into detail here, but I do recommend keeping it in mind for your use cases.

MLflow with whylogs

A tool that is much more oriented toward ML models in production is the `whylogs` open source Python library, which integrates with the WhyLabs app (`whylabsapp.com`). If you sign up for an account with WhyLabs, you can use their **application programming interface** (**API**) and send your model logging directly to their databases, where it will be analyzed and made accessible to you.

Neptune

A comparable tool is being delivered by Neptune (`neptune.ai`). The goal of Neptune is also to present an **ML operations** (**MLOps**) platform to which you can send your logging data from basically any Python (or other) model environment. After that, you can access the performance on their web platform, and all the heavy lifting for drift detection is taken off your shoulders.

You have now seen some theoretical methods for measuring and detecting drift, and some start-up platforms that are proposing to do this type of work for you if you do not have the capacity to deliver it. Still, we have not talked about something equally important, which is counteracting drift.

Counteracting drift

As discussed in the introduction, model drift is bound to happen. Maybe it happens very slowly or maybe it occurs quickly, but it is something that cannot really be avoided if we don't try to actively counteract it.

What you will realize in the coming section is that online learning, which has been covered extensively in this book, is actually a very performant method against drift. Although we had not yet clearly defined drift, you will now come to understand that online learning has a strong added value here.

We will now recapitulate two approaches for counteracting drift, depending on the type of work you are doing, as follows:

- Retraining for offline learning
- Online learning

Let's start with the most traditional case, which is offline learning with retraining strategies implemented against model decay.

Offline learning with retraining strategies against drift

Offline learning is still the most commonly used method for ML. In offline learning, the model is trained once and then used only for prediction. The following schematic diagram depicts the offline learning process:

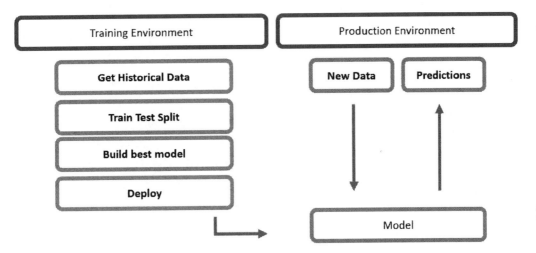

Figure 9.8 – Schematic diagram of offline learning

To update the model, it is generally necessary to retrain the full model and deploy a new version to your production environment. This is shown in *Figure 9.9*.

The advantages of this approach are that the model builder has complete control over their model. There is no risk of the model learning new—wrong—processes. This comes at the cost of not updating when data or concept drift occurs. In this way, its advantages and disadvantages are the opposite of online learning.

Online learning against drift

As you have seen throughout this book, online learning is an alternative to offline learning and allows the model to update whenever a new data point arrives. The following diagram illustrates how a retraining strategy works:

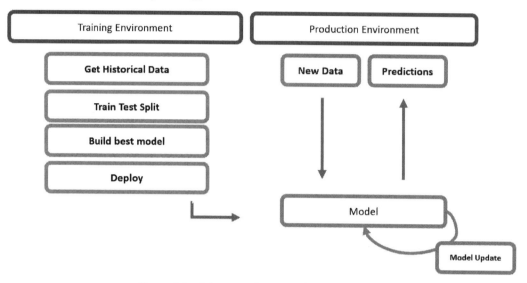

Figure 9.9 – Schematic diagram of online learning

Using online learning, the model has some autonomy in updating and will theoretically stay closer to the data: less drift should occur. However, this comes at a cost of the model builder not having full control over the theory model. Learning may go in the wrong direction, and unwanted decision rules are learned by the model.

The advantages are the opposite of offline learning, and it will really depend on the business case whether to choose online or offline learning.

Summary

In this chapter, you have first been introduced to the underlying foundations of model drift. You have seen that model drift and a decrease in model performance over time are to be expected in ML models in a real-life environment.

Decreasing performance can generally be attributed to drifting data, drifting concepts, or model-induced problems. Drifting data occurs when data measurements change over time, but the underlying theoretical concept behind the model stays the same. Concept drift captures problems of those theoretical underlying foundations of the learned processes.

Model- and model retraining-related problems are generally not considered standard reasons for drift, but they should still be monitored and taken seriously. Depending on your business case, relearning—especially if monitoring is lacking—can introduce large problems with ML systems.

Data drift can generally be measured well by using descriptive statistics. Concept drift is often harder to measure, but its presence can be deduced from an otherwise inexplicable decrease in model performance. In general, the importance here is not in attributing the decreasing performance to a specific cause, but rather in solving the problem using one of the provided solutions.

Retraining strategies can often be used for offline models. They are a way to update models, without giving up control of learned decision rules. Online models, as thoroughly presented throughout the earlier chapters of this book, are a great alternative to retraining offline models. The great advantage of using online models is that online models are made specifically for retraining. These models allow for a larger degree of autonomy and will prove useful in many business cases, as long as monitoring of both data and models is implemented correctly.

In the next chapter, you will see how to adapt **feature transformation (FT)** and scaling to the online modeling case. FT and scaling are standard practice in many ML use cases, but due to drift in data—and bias in windowing—it poses some theoretical difficulties that need to be taken into account.

Further reading

- Model drift: `https://www.ibm.com/cloud/watson-studio/drift`
- Data drift: `https://docs.microsoft.com/en-us/azure/machine-learning/how-to-monitor-datasets?tabs=python`
- Concept drift: `https://www.iguazio.com/blog/concept-drift-deep-dive-how-to-build-a-drift-aware-ml-system/`
- Dealing with concept drift: `https://neptune.ai/blog/concept-drift-best-practices`
- Retraining strategies: `https://www.kdnuggets.com/2019/12/ultimate-guide-model-retraining.html`

10
Feature Transformation and Scaling

In the previous chapter, you have seen how to manage drift and drift detection in streaming and online machine learning models. Drift detection, although not the main concept in machine learning, is a very important accessory aspect of machine learning in production.

Although many secondary topics are important in machine learning, some of the accessory topics are especially important with online models. Drift detection is particularly important, as the model's autonomy in relearning makes it slightly more black-box to the developer or data scientist. This has great advantages only as long as the retraining process is correctly managed by drift detection and comparable methods.

In this chapter, you will see another secondary machine learning topic that has important implications for online machine learning and streaming. Feature transformation and scaling are practices that are relatively well defined in traditional, batch machine learning. They do not generally pose any theoretical difficulty.

In online machine learning, scaling and feature transformation is not as straightforward. It is necessary to adapt the practice to the possibility that new data is not exactly comparable to the original data. This causes questions as to whether or not to refit feature transformations and scalers on every new piece of data arriving, but also on whether such practices will introduce bias into your already trained and continuously re-training models.

The topics that are covered in this chapter are as follows:

- Challenges of data preparation with streaming data
- Scaling data for streaming
- Transforming features in a streaming context

Technical requirements

You can find all the code for this book on GitHub at the following link: `https://github.com/PacktPublishing/Machine-Learning-for-Streaming-Data-with-Python`. If you are not yet familiar with Git and GitHub, the easiest way to download the notebooks and code samples is the following:

1. Go to the link of the repository.
2. Go to the green **Code** button.
3. Select **Download ZIP**.

When you download the ZIP file, unzip it in your local environment, and you will be able to access the code through your preferred Python editor.

Python environment

To follow along with this book, you can download the code in the repository and execute it using your preferred Python editor.

If you are not yet familiar with Python environments, I would advise you to check out Anaconda (`https://www.anaconda.com/products/individual`), which comes with Jupyter Notebook and JupyterLabs, which are both great for executing notebooks. It also comes with Spyder and VSCode for editing scripts and programs.

If you have difficulty installing Python or the associated programs on your machine, you can check out Google Colab (`https://colab.research.google.com/`) or Kaggle Notebooks (`https://www.kaggle.com/code`), which both allow you to run Python code in online notebooks for free, without any setup required.

> **Note**
> The code in the book will generally use Colab and Kaggle Notebooks
> with Python version *3.7.13*, and you can set up your own environment
> to mimic this.

Challenges of data preparation with streaming data

Before deep-diving into specific algorithms and solutions, let's first have a general discussion of why data preparation may be different when working with data that arrives in a streaming fashion. Multiple reasons can be identified, such as the following:

- The first, obvious issue is data drift. As discussed in much detail in the previous chapter, trends and descriptive statistics of your data can slowly change over time due to data drift. If your feature engineering or data preparation processes are too dependent on your data following certain distributions, you may run into problems when data drift occurs. As many solutions for this have been proposed in the previous chapter, this topic will be left out of consideration in the current chapter.

- The second issue is that population parameters are unknown. When observing data in a streaming fashion, it is possible, and even likely, that your estimates of the population parameters are slowly going to improve over time. As seen in *Chapter 3*, precision in your estimates of descriptive statistics will improve with the amount of data you have. When the descriptive statistic estimates are improving, the fact that they are changing over time does not make it easy to fix your formulas for data preparation, feature engineering, scaling, and the like:

  - As the first example of this, consider the range. The range represents the minimum and maximum values of the data that you observe. This is used extensively in data scaling and also in other algorithms. Now, imagine that the range (minimum and maximum values) in a batch can be different from the global range (global minimum and global maximum) of the data. After all, when new data arrives, you may observe a value that is higher or lower than anything observed in your historical data, just by the process of random sampling. Observing an observation that is higher than your maximum may cause an issue in scaling if you do not treat it right.

- ▪ Another example of this is when scaling with a normal distribution. The standard deviation and average in your batch may be different from the population standard deviation and population average. This may cause your scaler to behave differently after some time, which is a sort of data drift that is induced by your own scaling algorithm. Clearly, this must be avoided.

- • Many other cases of such problems exist, including observing new categories in a categorical value, which will lead to problems with your one-hot encoder or your models that use categorical variables. You can also imagine that occurring new types of values in your data such as NAs and InFs need to be managed well, rather than having them cause bugs. This is true in general, but when working with streaming, this tends to cause even more trouble than with regular data.

In the next section, we will learn what scaling is and how to work with it.

Scaling data for streaming

In the first part of this section, let's start by looking at some solutions for streaming scaling data. Before going into the solutions, let's do a quick recap of what scaling is and how it works.

Introducing scaling

Numerical variables can be of any scale, meaning they can have very high average values or low average values, for example. Some machine learning algorithms are not at all impacted by the scale of a variable, whereas other machine learning algorithms can be strongly impacted.

Scaling is the practice of taking a numerical variable and reducing its range, and potentially its standard deviation, to a pre-specified range. This will allow all machine learning algorithms to learn from the data without problems.

Scaling with MinMaxScaler

To achieve this goal, a commonly used method is the Min-Max scaler. The Min-Max scaler will take an input variable in any range and reduce all of the values to fall in between the range (0 to 1), meaning that the minimum value of the scaled variable will be 0 and the maximum of the scaled variable will be 1. Sometimes, an alternative is used in which the minimum is not 0, but -1.

The mathematical formula for Min-Max scaling is the following:

$$X_{scaled} = \frac{X - X_{min}}{X_{max} - X_{min}}$$

Scaling with StandardScaler

Another very common approach to scaling is standardizing. Standardizing is a method strongly based on statistics, which allows you to take any variable and take it back to a standard normal distribution. The standard normal distribution has an average of 0 and a standard deviation of 1.

The mathematical formula for the StandardScaler is the following:

$$X_{scaled} = \frac{X - mean(X)}{stdev(X)}$$

The values of the scaled variable will not be in any specific range; the new value of the scaled variable represents the number of standard deviations that the original value is away from the original mean. A very extreme value (imagine four or five standard deviations away from the mean) would have a value of four or five, which by the way can be both positive and negative.

Choosing your scaling method

The choice of scaling algorithm depends on the use case, and it is generally a good idea to do tuning of your machine learning pipeline in which different scaling methods are used with different algorithms. After all, the choice of scaling method has an impact on the performance of the training of the method.

The Min-Max scaler is known to have difficulty with outliers. After all, a very extreme outlier would be set to the maximum value, that is, to 1. Then, this may cause the other values to be reduced to a much smaller range.

The StandardScaler deals with this in a better way, as the outliers would still be outliers and simply take on high values in the scaled variable. This can be a disadvantage at the same time, mainly when you are using machine learning algorithms that need the values to be between 0 and 1.

Adapting scaling to a streaming context

Let's now have a look at how we can adapt each of those approaches to the case of streaming data. We'll start with the Min-Max scaler.

Adapting the MinMaxScaler to streaming

The MinMaxScaler works perfectly on a fixed dataset. It guarantees that the values of the scaled data will be between 0 and 1, just as required by some machine learning algorithms. However, in the case of streaming data, this is much less easy to manage.

When new data arrives one by one (in a stream), it is impossible to decide on the minimum or maximum value. After all, you cannot expect one value to be both minimum and maximum. The same problem occurs when batching: there is no guarantee that the batch maximum is higher than the global maximum, and the same for the minimum.

You could use the training data to decide on the minimum and the maximum, but then the problem is that your new data could be above the training maximum or below the training minimum. This would result in the scaled values being outside of the range (0 to 1).

A solution for this is to use a running minimum and a running maximum. This means that you continue updating the MinMaxScaler so that every time a lower minimum is observed, you update the minimum in the MinMaxScaler formula, and every time a higher maximum is observed, you update the maximum.

The advantage of this method is that it guarantees that your scaled data will always be between 0 and 1. A disadvantage is that the first values for training the MinMaxScaler will be scaled quite badly. This is easily solved by using some training data to initialize the MinMaxScaler. Outliers can also be a problem, as having one very extreme value will strongly affect the MinMaxScaler's formula, and scores will be very different after that. This could be solved by using an outlier detection method as described extensively in *Chapter 5*.

Let's now move on to a Python implementation of an adaptive MinMaxScaler:

1. For this, we will use the implementation of the MinMaxScaler in the Python library, `River`. We will use the following data for this example:

Code Block 10-1

```
import numpy as np
data = np.random.randint(0, 100, size=1000)
```

2. The histogram of this data can be created using the following code:

Code Block 10-2

```
import matplotlib.pyplot as plt
plt.hist(data)
```

The resulting histogram looks like the following:

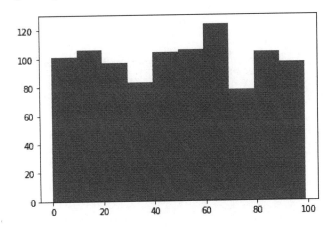

Figure 10.1 – Resulting histogram of Code Block 10-2

3. Now, to scale this data, let's use the `MinMaxScaler` function from River. Looping through the data will simulate the data arriving in a streaming fashion, and the use of the `learn_one` method shows that the data is updated step by step:

Code Block 10-3

```
!pip install river
from river import preprocessing
# convert the data to required format
data_stream = [{'x':float(x)} for x in list(data)]

# initialize list for scaled values
data_scaled = []

# initialize scaler
my_scaler = preprocessing.MinMaxScaler()
```

```
# streaming
for observation in data_stream:

    # learn (update)
    my_scaler.learn_one(observation)

    # scale the observation
    scaled_obs = my_scaler.transform_one(observation)

    # store the scaled result
    data_scaled.append(scaled_obs['x'])
```

4. Now, it will be interesting to see the histogram of the scaled data. It can be created as follows:

Code Block 10-4

```
import matplotlib.pyplot as plt
plt.hist(data_scaled)
```

The histogram is shown in the following:

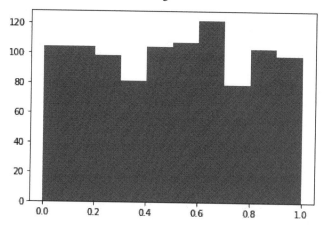

Figure 10.2 – Resulting histogram of Code Block 10-4

This histogram clearly shows that we have been successful in scaling the data into the 0 to 1 range.

Now that you have seen the theory and implementation of the MinMaxScaler, let's now see the StandardScaler, a common alternative to this method.

Adapting the Standard Scaler to streaming

The problem that may occur in standard scaling when observing more extreme data in the future, is not exactly the same problem as the one that is seen in Min-Max scaling. Where the Min-Max scaler uses the minimum and the maximum to compute the scaling method, the standard scaler uses the mean and standard deviation.

The reason why this is very different is that the minimum and maximum are relatively likely to be surpassed at one point in time. This would result in the scaled values being higher than 1 or lower than 0, which may pose real problems for your machine learning algorithms.

In the standard scaler, any extreme values occurring in the future will impact your estimate of the global mean and standard deviation, but they are much less likely to impact them very severely. After all, the mean and the standard deviation are much less sensitive to the observation of a small number of extreme values.

Given this theoretical consideration, you may conclude that it isn't really necessary to update the standard scaler. However, it may be best to update it anyway, as this is a good way to keep your machine learning methods up to date. The added value of this will be less impacting than when using the Min-Max scaler, but it is a best practice to do it anyway.

One solution that you can use is to use the AdaptiveStandardScaler in the `Riverml` package. It uses an exponentially-weighted running mean and variance to make sure that slight drifts of the normal distribution of your data are taken into account without having it weigh too strongly. Let's see a Python example of how to use the AdaptiveStandardScaler:

1. We will use the following data for this example:

Code Block 10-5

```
import numpy as np
data = np.random.normal(12, 15, size=1000)
```

2. This data follows a normal distribution, as you can see from the histogram. You can create a histogram as follows:

Code Block 10-6

```
import matplotlib.pyplot as plt
plt.hist(data)
```

The resulting histogram is shown here:

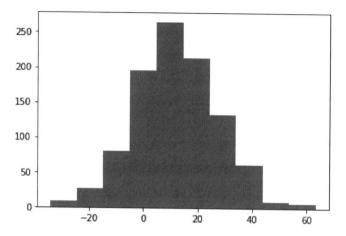

Figure 10.3 – Resulting histogram of Code Block 10-6

The data clearly follows a normal distribution, but it is not centered around 0 and it is not standardized to a standard deviation of 1.

3. Now, to scale this data, let's use StandardScaler from River. Again, we will loop through the data to simulate streaming. Also, we again use the learn_one method to update the data step by step:

Code Block 10-7

```
from river import preprocessing

# convert the data to required format
data_stream = [{'x':float(x)} for x in list(data)]

# initialize list for scaled values
data_scaled = []

# initialize scaler
my_scaler = preprocessing.StandardScaler()

# streaming
for observation in data_stream:

    # learn (update)
```

```
my_scaler.learn_one(observation)

# scale the observation
scaled_obs = my_scaler.transform_one(observation)

# store the scaled result
data_scaled.append(scaled_obs['x'])
```

4. To verify that it has worked correctly, let's redo the histogram using the following code:

Code Block 10-8

```
plt.hist(data_scaled)
```

The histogram is shown here:

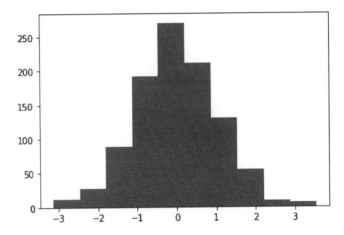

Figure 10.4 – Resulting histogram of Code Block 10-8

As you can see, the data is clearly centered around 0, and the new, scaled value indicates the number of standard deviations that each data point is away from the mean.

In the next section, you will see how to adapt feature transformation in a streaming context.

Transforming features in a streaming context

Scaling data is a way of pre-processing data for machine learning, but many other statistical methods can be used for data preparation. In this second part of this chapter let's deep dive into the **principal component analysis (PCA)** method, a much-used method for preparing data at the beginning of any machine learning.

Introducing PCA

PCA is a machine learning method that can be used for multiple applications. When working with highly multivariate data, PCA can be used in an interpretative way, where you use it to make sense of and analyze multivariate datasets. This is a use of PCA in data analysis.

Another way to use PCA is to prepare data for machine learning. From a high-level point of view, PCA could be seen as an alternative to scaling that reduces the number of variables of your data to make it easier for the model to fit. This is the use of PCA that is most relevant for the current chapter, and this is how it will be used in the example.

Mathematical definition of PCA

PCA works on multivariate data (or data with multiple columns). These columns generally have a business definition. The goal of PCA is to keep all information in the data but change the current variable definitions into variables with different interpretations.

The new variables are called the **principal components**, and they are found in such a way that the first component contains the most possible variation, and the second component is the component that is orthogonal to the first one and explains the most variation possible while being orthogonal.

A schematical overview is shown here:

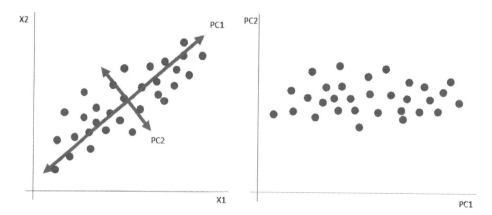

Figure 10.5 – Schematic overview of PCA

This example clearly shows how the original data on the left is transformed into principal components on the right. The first principal component has much more value in terms of information than any of the original variables. When working with hundreds of variables, you can imagine that you will need to retain only a limited number of components (based on different criteria and your use case), which may make it easier for your machine learning algorithm to learn from the data.

Regular PCA in Python

To have a good comparison between regular and incremental PCA, it is good to get everybody up to speed and do a quick example of a regular PCA first:

1. To do this, let's create some simulated sample data to work on the example. We can make a small example dataset as follows:

Code Block 10-9

```
import numpy as np
import pandas as pd


X1 = np.random.normal(5, 1, size=100)
X2 = np.random.normal(5, 0.5, size=100)
data = pd.DataFrame({'X1': X1, 'X2': X1 + X2})
data.head()
```

The data looks like this:

	X1	X2
0	4.179122	9.900635
1	4.432070	9.447144
2	4.418185	9.302935
3	6.114153	10.812437
4	4.854368	10.100938

Figure 10.6 – The resulting data

2. You can make a plot of this data as follows:

Code Block 10-10

```
import matplotlib.pyplot as plt
plt.scatter(data['X1'], data['X2'])
```

The scatter plot shows a plot that is quite similar to the sketch in the earlier schematic drawing:

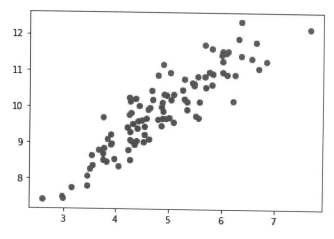

Figure 10.7 – The resulting image of Code Block 10-10

3. Let's now use a regular PCA to identify the components and transform the data. The following block of code shows how to fit a PCA using scikit-learn:

Code Block 10-11

```
from sklearn.decomposition import PCA
my_pca = PCA()
transformed_data = my_pca.fit_transform(data)
transformed_data = pd.DataFrame(transformed_
data, columns = ['PC1', 'PC2'])
transformed_data.head()
```

The transformed data looks as follows:

	PC1	PC2
0	0.598106	-0.515128
1	0.757523	-0.020939
2	0.872506	0.067196
3	-1.388008	0.279275
4	-0.008712	-0.157566

Figure 10.8 – The transformed data

4. We can plot it just like we did with the previous data. This can be done using the following code:

Code Block 10-12

```
plt.scatter(transformed_data['PC1'], transformed_data['PC2'])
plt.xlim(-4, 4)
plt.ylim(-4, 4)
plt.show()
```

The plot looks as follows:

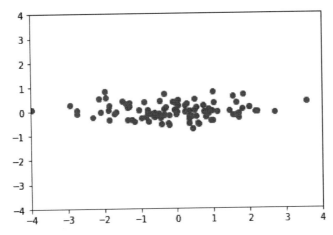

Figure 10.9 – Plot of the transformed data

You can clearly see that this looks a lot like the resulting plot in the earlier theoretical introduction. This PCA has successfully identified the first principal component to be the component that explains the largest part of the data. The second component explains the largest part of the remaining data (after the first component).

Incremental PCA for streaming

PCA, in a streaming context, cannot be easily calculated on individual data points. After all, you can imagine that it is impossible to determine the standard deviation of a single data point, and therefore, there is no possible way to determine the best components.

The proposed solution is to do this through batches and to compute your PCA in batches rather than all at once. The scikit-learn package has a functionality called IncrementalPCA, which allows you to fit PCA in batches. Let's use the following code for fitting IncrementalPCA on the same data as before and compare the results. The code to fit and transform using IncrementalPCA is shown in the following:

Code Block 10-13

```
from sklearn.decomposition import IncrementalPCA
my_incremental_pca = IncrementalPCA(batch_size = 10)
transformed_data_2 = my_incremental_pca.fit_transform(data)
transformed_data_2 = pd.DataFrame(transformed_
data_2, columns = ['PC1', 'PC2'])
transformed_data_2.head()
```

The transformed data using this second method looks as follows:

	PC1	PC2
0	-0.598106	-0.515128
1	-0.757523	-0.020939
2	-0.872506	0.067196
3	1.388008	0.279275
4	0.008712	-0.157566

Figure 10.10 – The transformed data using incremental PCA

Now, let's also make a plot of this data to see whether this batch-wise PCA was successful in fitting the real components, or whether it is far away from the original PCA:

Code Block 10-14

```
plt.scatter(transformed_data_2['PC1'], transformed_
data_2['PC2'])
plt.xlim(-4, 4)
plt.ylim(-4, 4)
plt.show()
```

The resulting scatter plot is shown in the following:

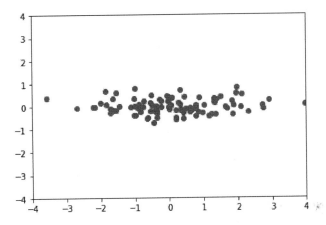

Figure 10.11 – The scatter plot of the transformed data using incremental PCA

This scatter plot shows that the PCA has been correctly fitted. Do not be confused by the fact that the incremental PCA has inversed the first component (the image is mirrored left to right compared to the preceding one). This is not wrong but just mirrored. This incremental PCA has captured the two components very well.

Summary

In this chapter, you have seen some common methods for data preparation being adapted to streaming and online data. For streaming data, it is important to have easily refitting or re-estimating models.

In the first part of the chapter, you have seen two methods for scaling. The MinMaxScaler scales the data to the 0 to 1 range and, therefore, needs to make sure that none of the new data points get outside of this range. The StandardScaler uses a statistical normalization process using the mean and standard deviation.

The second part of the chapter demonstrated a regular PCA and a new, incremental version called IncrementalPCA. This incremental method allows you to fit PCA in batches, which can help you when fitting PCA on streaming data.

With scaling and feature transformation in this chapter, and drift detection in the previous chapter, you have already seen a good part of the auxiliary tasks of machine learning on streaming. In the coming chapter, you will see the third and last secondary topic to machine learning and streaming, which is catastrophic forgetting: an impactful problem that can occur in online machine learning, causing the model to forget important learned trends. The chapter will explain how to detect and avoid it.

Further reading

- *MinMaxScaler in River*: https://riverml.xyz/latest/api/preprocessing/MinMaxScaler/

- *StandardScaler in River*: https://riverml.xyz/latest/api/preprocessing/StandardScaler/

- *PCA in scikit-learn*: https://scikit-learn.org/stable/modules/generated/sklearn.decomposition.PCA.html

- *Incremental PCA in scikit-learn*: https://scikit-learn.org/stable/modules/generated/sklearn.decomposition.IncrementalPCA.html

11
Catastrophic Forgetting

In the previous two chapters, we started to look at a number of auxiliary tasks for online machine learning and working with streaming data. *Chapter 9* covered drift detection and solutions and *Chapter 10* covered feature transformation and scaling in a streaming context. The current chapter introduces a third and final topic to this list of auxiliary tasks, namely catastrophic forgetting.

Catastrophic forgetting, also known as catastrophic interference, is the tendency of machine learning models to forget what they have learned upon new updates, wrongly de-learning correctly learned older tendencies as new tendencies are learned from new data.

As you have seen a lot of examples of online models throughout this book, you will understand that continuous updating of the models creates a large risk of this learning going wrong. It has already been touched upon briefly, in the chapter on drift and drift detection, that model learning going wrong can also be seen as a real risk of performance degradation.

Drift, however, tends to be used for pointing out drift in either the independent variables (data drift) or in the relations between independent variables and dependent variables (concept drift). As catastrophic forgetting is really a problem inside the coefficients of the model, we could not really consider catastrophic forgetting to be a part of drift.

Machine learning models, especially online machine learning models, are often used in a relatively black-box manner, meaning that we look at their outcomes but do not necessarily spend much time looking at the inside mechanisms. This becomes a problem when detecting wrongly learned patterns. Machine learning explicability is therefore also related to the topic of catastrophic forgetting and will be covered as well.

This chapter will cover the problem of machine learning models updating in the wrong manner, which we call catastrophic forgetting or catastrophic inference, with the following chapters being covered:

- Defining catastrophic forgetting

- Detection of catastrophic forgetting

- Model explicability versus catastrophic forgetting

Technical requirements

You can find all the code for this book on GitHub at the following link: `https://github.com/PacktPublishing/Machine-Learning-for-Streaming-Data-with-Python`. If you are not yet familiar with Git and GitHub, the easiest way to download the notebooks and code samples is the following:

1. Go to the link of the repository.

2. Go to the green **Code** button.

3. Select **Download zip**.

When you download the ZIP file, you unzip it in your local environment, and you will be able to access the code through your preferred Python editor.

Python environment

To follow along with this book, you can download the code in the repository and execute it using your preferred Python editor.

If you are not yet familiar with Python environments, I would advise you to check out either Anaconda (`https://www.anaconda.com/products/individual`), which comes with the Jupyter Notebook and JupyterLab, which are both great for executing notebooks. It also comes with Spyder and VS Code for editing scripts and programs.

If you have difficulty installing Python or the associated programs on your machine, you can check out Google Colab (`https://colab.research.google.com/`) or Kaggle Notebooks (`https://www.kaggle.com/code`), which both allow you to run Python code in online notebooks for free, without any setup.

> **Note**
> The code in the book will generally use Colab and Kaggle Notebooks with Python version 3.7.13 and you can set up your own environment to mimic this.

Introducing catastrophic forgetting

Catastrophic forgetting was initially defined as a problem that occurs on (deep) neural networks. Deep neural networks are a set of very complex machine learning models that, thanks to their extreme complexity, are able to learn very complex patterns. Of course, this is the case only when there is enough data.

Neural networks have been studied for multiple decades. They used to be mathematically interesting but practically infeasible to execute due to the lack of computing power. The current-day progress in computing power has made it possible for neural networks to gain the popularity that they are currently observing.

The complexity of neural networks also makes them sensitive to the problem of catastrophic forgetting. The way a neural network learns (from a high point of view) is by making many update passes to the coefficients and at every update, the model should fit a little bit better to the data. A schematic overview of a neural network's parameters can be seen here:

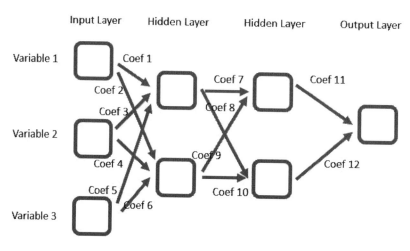

Figure 11.1 – Schematic overview of the number of coefficients in a neural network

In this schematic drawing, you see that even for a very small neural network there are many coefficients. The larger the number of nodes becomes, the larger the number of parameters to estimate. When comparing this to traditional statistical methods, you can see that the idea of making so many passes is relatively different and causes different problems than those that were common in traditional statistics.

Catastrophic forgetting is one such problem. It was first observed in a study in 1989, in which an experiment was presented. This experiment trained neural networks on the task of doing additions (from 1 + 1 = 2 to 1 + 9 = 10). A sequential method was tested, in which the model first learned only the first task, and then a new task was added once the first one was mastered.

The conclusion of this and other experiments was that adding new tasks after the first one has been learned will cause interference with the original learned model. They observed that the newer information has to be learned, the larger this disruption will be. Finally, they found out that the problem occurs in sequential learning only. If you learn all tasks at the same time, there is not really any re-learning happening so forgetting cannot really happen.

For more detailed, scientific resources on catastrophic forgetting in the specific case of online learning using neural networks, I recommend checking out the two links here:

- `https://proceedings.neurips.cc/paper/2021/file/54ee290e805 89a2a1225c338a71839f5-Paper.pdf`
- `https://www.cs.uic.edu/~liub/lifelong-learning/continual-learning.pdf`

Let's now see how catastrophic forgetting affects online models in general.

Catastrophic forgetting in online models

Although catastrophic forgetting was initially identified as a problem for neural networks, you can imagine that online machine learning has the same problem of continuous re-learning. The problem of catastrophic forgetting, or catastrophic inference, is therefore also present and needs to be mastered.

If models are updated at every new data point, it is expected that coefficients will change over time. Yet as modern-day machine learning algorithms are very complex and have huge numbers of coefficients or trees, it is a fairly difficult task to keep a close eye on them.

In an ideal world, the most beneficial goal would probably be to try and avoid any wrong learning in your machine learning at all. One way to do this is to keep a close eye on model performance and keep tight versioning systems in place to make sure that even if your model is wrongly learning anything, it does not get deployed in a production system. We will go into this topic shortly.

Another solution that is possible is to work with drift detection methods, as you saw in Chapter 9. When you closely follow your model's performance and the distributions of your data, and other KPIs and descriptive statistics, you should be able to detect problems rather soon, which will allow you to intervene rapidly.

As a third tool for managing catastrophic forgetting, you will see more tools for model explicability in this chapter. One of the problems of catastrophic forgetting is that the models are too much of a black box. Using tools from the domain of model explicability will help you to have a peek inside those black-box models. This will allow you to detect catastrophic forgetting and catastrophic inference based more on business logic rather than technical logic. The combination of business and technical logic together will be a strong combination to prepare against catastrophic forgetting.

Detecting catastrophic forgetting

In this chapter, we are going to look at two different approaches that you could use to detect catastrophic forgetting. The first approach is to implement a system that can detect problems with a model just after it has learned something. To do this, we are going to implement a Python example in multiple steps:

1. Develop a model training loop with online learning.

2. Add direct evaluation to this model.

3. Add longer-term evaluation to this model.

4. Add a system to avoid model updating in case of wrong learning.

Using Python to detect catastrophic forgetting

To work through this example, let's start by implementing an online regression model, just like you have already seen earlier on in this book:

1. To do this, we first need to generate some data. The code to generate the data for this example is shown here:

Code Block 11-1

```python
import random
X = [
     1, 1, 1, 2, 2, 2, 3, 3, 3, 4, 4, 4, 5, 5, 5,
     6, 6, 6, 7, 7, 7, 8, 8, 8, 9, 9, 9, 10, 10, 10
]
y = [
     x + random.random() for x in X[:15]] +
     [x * 2 + random.random() for x in X[15:]
]
```

If you look at this code, you can see that there is a shift occurring in the pattern. In the first 15 observations, y is defined as x + random.randint(), meaning just the same value as x but with some random variation. After the 15th observation, this shift changes and becomes x * 2 + random.randint, meaning the double of x with some added random variation. This example will be perfect to see how a model needs to update with time.

2. Let's now make a quick plot of this data to have a better idea of what this shift actually looks like. This can be done with the code that is shown here:

Code Block 11-2

```
import matplotlib.pyplot as plt

plt.scatter(X, y)
```

The resulting graph is shown here:

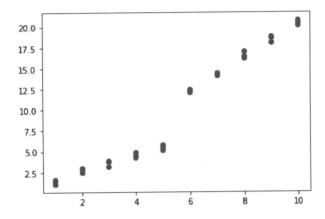

Figure 11.2 – The scatter plot resulting from the preceding code block

The first linear trend clearly holds from x = 1 to x = 5, but a different, steeper function starts at x = 6 and goes on to x = 10.

3. We are going to use River in this example, so it will be necessary to get the data in the right format. You should by now have mastered the data formats for the River library, but you can refer to the following code if necessary:

Code Block 11-3

```
X_dict = [{'X': x} for x in X]

for X_i, y_i in zip(X_dict, y):
  print(X_i, y_i)
```

The result of this code block should be something like the following:

```
{'X': 1} 1.6127106272891965
{'X': 1} 1.5216679385964245
{'X': 1} 1.0883010537681848
{'X': 2} 2.973263598415156
{'X': 2} 2.8064049061561525
{'X': 2} 2.4725052887411096
{'X': 3} 3.839774377317677
{'X': 3} 3.75067740887802186
{'X': 3} 3.126953050185566
{'X': 4} 4.301619856107971
{'X': 4} 4.89816859982475
{'X': 4} 4.43260657750843
{'X': 5} 5.554334186506866
{'X': 5} 5.140354483630828
{'X': 5} 5.7831002321588825
{'X': 6} 12.446648917034642
{'X': 6} 12.146837622160884
{'X': 6} 12.084217492938837
{'X': 7} 14.1100279960006409
{'X': 7} 14.377786454513041
{'X': 7} 14.215506502534183
{'X': 8} 16.39641074624865
{'X': 8} 16.978811207844867
{'X': 8} 16.149872306001697
{'X': 9} 18.649937189225014
{'X': 9} 18.112306721897507
{'X': 9} 18.71640496965094
{'X': 10} 20.45275258199673
{'X': 10} 20.722114535933514
{'X': 10} 20.13493050382043
```

Figure 11.3 – The output resulting from the preceding code block

4. Now, let's add a `KNNRegressor` function from the River library to this loop, and at each new data point, use the `learn_one` method to update the model. This is done using the following code:

Code Block 11-4

```
!pip install river
from river.neighbors import KNNRegressor
my_knn = KNNRegressor(window_size=3)


X_dict = [{'X': x} for x in X]
```

```
for X_i, y_i in zip(X_dict, y):
  my_knn.learn_one(X_i, y_i)
```

5. We can compute the final training error of this model to have a general idea of the amount of errors that we should expect. The following code does exactly that:

Code Block 11-4

```
preds = []
for X_i in X_dict:
  preds.append(my_knn.predict_one(X_i))

sum_absolute_error = 0
for pred, real in zip(preds, y):
  sum_absolute_error += abs(pred - real)

mean_absolute_error = sum_absolute_error / len(preds)
print(mean_absolute_error)
```

In the current example, this computes a mean absolute error of 10.

6. Let's now have a more detailed look into the step-by-step learning quality of the model. We can do this by using continuous evaluation. This means that every time we learn, we will evaluate the model:

Code Block 11-5

```
my_knn = KNNRegressor(window_size=3)

X_dict = [{'X': x} for x in X]

step_by_step_error = []
for i in range(len(X_dict)):
  my_knn.learn_one(X_dict[i], y[i])
  abs_error = abs(my_knn.predict_one(X_dict[i]) - y[i])
  step_by_step_error.append(abs_error)
```

7. The following code will plot those errors over time to see how the model is learning:

Code Block 11-6

```
plt.plot(step_by_step_error)
```

The following plot results from this code:

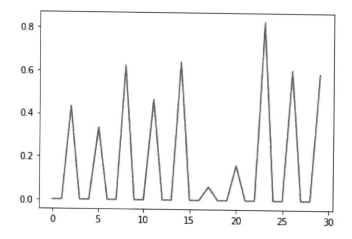

Figure 11.4 – The plot resulting from the preceding code block

Interestingly, the model seems to obtain a perfect score every time that we see a new value for x, then the second time that the same x value occurs, we have a perfect score again, but the third time, we have a larger error!

8. It would be great to compare this with the final error, which was not computed step by step but just at once, using the following code:

Code Block 11-7

```
preds = []
for X_i in X_dict:
    preds.append(my_knn.predict_one(X_i))

all_errors = []
for pred, real in zip(preds, y):
    all_errors.append(abs(pred - real))

plt.plot(step_by_step_error)
```

```
plt.plot(all_errors)
plt.show()
```

The output from this code block is shown hereafter:

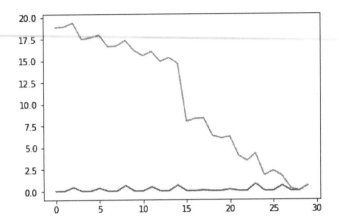

Figure 11.5 – The plot resulting from the preceding code block

You can clearly observe that when evaluating the model step by step, the error on each data point does not seem too big. However, when evaluating all at the end, you see that the model has actually forgotten the first data points! This is a good example of how catastrophic forgetting can be observed in practice.

9.   As a final step, let's add a small evaluation to the model loop to help you in realizing that the model has forgotten your first scores:

Code Block 11-8

```
my_knn = KNNRegressor(window_size=3)

X_dict = [{'X': x} for x in X]

step_by_step_error = []

for i in range(len(X_dict)):
    my_knn.learn_one(X_dict[i], y[i])
    abs_error = abs(my_knn.predict_one(X_dict[i]) - y[i])
    step_by_step_error.append(abs_error)

    all_errors_recomputed = []
```

```
for j in range(i):
    orig_error = step_by_step_error[j]
    after_error = abs(my_knn.predict_one(X_
dict[j]) - y[j])
    if after_error > orig_error:
        print(f'At learn-
ing step {i}, data point {j} was partly forgotten')
```

In this code block, a rule was made to detect forgetting as soon as the error was larger than the original error. Of course, this is a really severe detection mechanism, and you could imagine other approaches in the place of this one. For example, this could be a percentage change or an absolute number that must not be surpassed. This all depends on your business case.

Now that you have seen an approach for detecting catastrophic forgetting using alarm mechanisms based on model performance, let's go on to the next part of this chapter, in which you'll see how to use model explicability to detect catastrophic forgetting.

Model explicability versus catastrophic forgetting

Looking at model performance is generally a good way to keep track of your model and it will definitely help you to detect that something, somewhere in the model, has gone wrong. Generally, this will be enough of an alerting mechanism and will help you to manage your models in production.

If you want to understand exactly what has gone wrong, however, you'll need to dig deeper into your model. Looking at performance only is more of a black-box approach, whereas we can also extract things such as trees, coefficients, variable importance, and the like to see what has actually changed inside the model.

There is no one-size-fits-all method for deep diving into models. All model categories have their own specific method for fitting the data, and an inspection of their fit would therefore be strongly dependent on the model itself. In the remainder of this section, however, we will look at two very common structures in machine learning: linear models with coefficients and trees.

Explaining models using linear coefficients

In this first example, we'll build a linear regression on some sample data and extract coefficients of the model to give an interpretation of them:

1. You can create the data for this example using the following code:

Code Block 11-9

```
import pandas as pd
ice_cream_sales = [10, 9, 8, 7, 6, 5, 4, 3, 2 , 1]
degrees_celsius = [30, 25, 20, 19, 18, 17, 15, 13, 10, 5]
price  = [2,2, 3, 3, 4, 4, 5, 5, 6, 6]

data = pd.DataFrame({
    'ice_cream_sales': ice_cream_sales,
    'degrees_celsius': degrees_celsius,
    'price': price
})

data
```

The data is shown here in a dataframe format:

	ice_cream_sales	degrees_celcius	price
0	10	30	2
1	9	25	2
2	8	20	3
3	7	19	3
4	6	18	4
5	5	17	4
6	4	15	5
7	3	13	5
8	2	10	6
9	1	5	6

Figure 11.6 – The plot resulting from the preceding code block

2. Let's create two scatter plots to have a better visual idea of how ice cream sales are related to temperature and price (in this fictitious example). The following code shows how to create the first scatter plot:

Code Block 11-10

```
plt.scatter(data['degrees_celsius'], data['ice_cream_
sales'])
```

This results in the following graph:

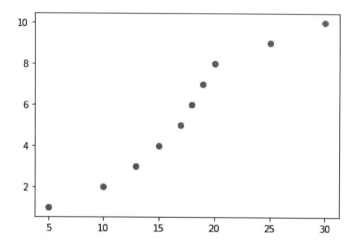

Figure 11.7 – The plot resulting from the preceding code block

3. The second scatter plot can be created as follows:

Code Block 11-11

```
plt.scatter(data['price'], data['ice_cream_sales'])
```

This results in the following graph:

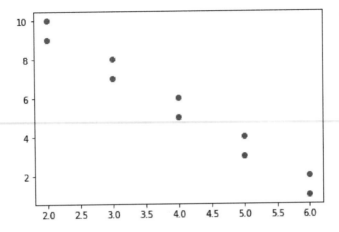

Figure 11.8 – The plot resulting from the preceding code block

You can clearly see that sales are higher when the temperature is higher, and sales are lower when the temperature is lower. Also, higher prices are correlated with lower sales, and lower prices are correlated with higher sales.

4.   These are two logical and explainable factors in ice cream sales, but this is not yet a model. Let's use a `LinearRegression` function to model this straightforward linear relationship:

Code Block 11-12

```
from sklearn.linear_model import LinearRegression
my_lr = LinearRegression()
my_lr.fit(X = data[['degrees_
celsius', 'price']], y = data['ice_cream_sales'])
```

5.   We can evaluate the (in-sample) fit of this model as follows:

Code Block 11-13

```
from sklearn.metrics import r2_score
r2_score(data['ice_cream_sales'], my_
lr.predict(data[['degrees_celsius', 'price']]))
```

This model yields a training R2 score of 0.98, meaning that the model fits really well to the training data.

6. We are now at the step where we need to go deeper into the model than just looking at performance. With the linear regression, we need to look at coefficients to be able to interpret what they have fitted. The coefficients are extracted in the following code:

Code Block 11-14

```
pd.DataFrame({'variable': ['degrees_
celsius', 'price'], 'coefficient': my_lr.coef_})
```

This gives the following output:

	variable	coefficient
0	degrees_celcius	0.153677
1	price	-1.300768

Figure 11.9 – The coefficients resulting from the preceding code block

You can interpret this as follows:

- Every additional degree Celsius will increase ice cream sales by 0.15, given a constant price.

- Every euro added to the price will decrease ice cream sales by 1.3, given a constant temperature.

Explaining models using dendrograms

While looking at coefficients is great for linear models, some models do not have any coefficients. Examples of this are basically any models that use trees. Trees have nodes and these nodes are split based on yes/no questions. Although you cannot extract coefficients from trees, the advantage is that you can simply print out the entire tree as a graph! We'll look at that in the next example:

1. To get started, we need to fit a `DecisionTreeRegressor` function on the same data as the one we used before, using the following code:

Code Block 11-15

```
from sklearn.tree import DecisionTreeRegressor
my_dt = DecisionTreeRegressor()
my_dt.fit(X = data[['degrees_
celsius', 'price']], y = data['ice_cream_sales'])
```

2. To get a general idea whether the model fits, let's compute an R2 score on the training set, just like we did before:

Code Block 11-16

```
r2_score(data['ice_cream_sales'], my_
dt.predict(data[['degrees_celsius', 'price']]))
```

The result is 1.0, which means that the decision tree has obtained a perfect fit on the training data. Nothing guarantees that this will generalize out-of-sample, but that is not necessarily a problem for explaining the model.

3. To extract the tree as an image, you can simply use the code here:

Code Block 11-17

```
import sklearn
plt.figure(figsize=(15,15))
sklearn.tree.plot_tree(my_dt)
plt.show()
```

This will print out the entire tree and give you perfect insight into how the predictions have been made:

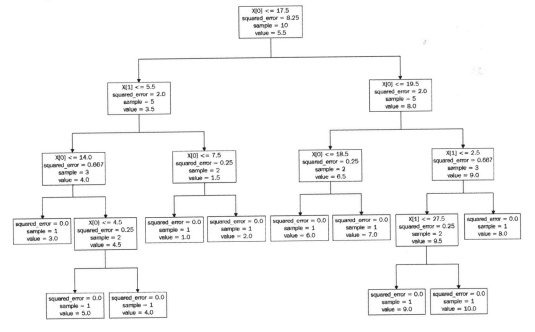

Figure 11.10 – The resulting dendrogram from the preceding code block

Explaining models using variable importance

As a third and final method for explaining models, you can look at variable importance. Again, this is something that will not work for all machine learning models. Yet, for rather complex models it is often too difficult to look at all dendrograms and variable importance estimates are a great replacement for this.

Let's extract the variable importance from the decision tree model that was built previously. This can be done using the following code:

Code Block 11-18

```
pd.DataFrame({'variable': ['degrees_
celsius', 'price'], 'importance': my_dt.feature_importances_})
```

The resulting dataframe looks as follows:

	variable	importance
0	degrees_celcius	0.884848
1	price	0.115152

Figure 11.11 – The importance value

This tells us that the decision tree has used degrees Celsius more than it has used the price as a predictor variable.

Summary

In this chapter, you have seen how catastrophic forgetting can cause bad performance in your model, especially when data arrives in a sequential manner. Especially when one trend is learned first and a second trend follows, the risk of forgetting the first trend is real and needs to be controlled.

Although there is no one-stop solution for these issues, there are many things that can be done to avoid bad models from going into production systems. You have seen how to implement continuous evaluation metrics and you have seen how you would be able to detect that some trends have been forgotten.

Performance-based metrics are great for detecting problems but are not able to tell you what exactly has gone wrong inside the model. You have seen three methods of model explanation that can help you deep-dive further into most models. By extracting from the model which trends or relationships the model has learned, you can identify whether this corresponds to an already known business logic or common sense.

In the next and final chapter of this book, we will conclude the different topics that have been presented and consider a number of best practices to keep in mind while working on online models and streaming data.

Further reading

- KNNRegressor: `https://riverml.xyz/latest/api/neighbors/KNNRegressor/`

- LinearRegression: `https://scikit-learn.org/stable/modules/generated/sklearn.linear_model.LinearRegression.html`

- DecisionTree: `https://scikit-learn.org/stable/modules/generated/sklearn.tree.DecisionTreeRegressor.html`

- Tree_plot: `https://scikit-learn.org/stable/modules/generated/sklearn.tree.plot_tree.html`

12
Conclusion and Best Practices

Throughout the chapters of this book, you have been introduced to the field of machine learning on streaming data, using mainly online models. In this last chapter, it is time for a recapitulative overview of all that has been seen throughout the eleven earlier chapters of the book.

This chapter will cover the following:

- Best practices to keep in mind
- Next steps for your learning journey
- Best practices

Practice is always different from theory. You have seen a lot of theoretical knowledge throughout this book. In this final section, you will see a number of best practices that always need to be kept in mind while applying the theory in real-life use cases:

1. **Clean data/data quality**

   Data quality and problems with data understanding are daily problems in most companies. The famous saying goes: "Garbage in, garbage out," implying that when you do machine learning on garbage data, your outputs will also be useless. Thorough data exploration needs to be done on any new business case that comes to you, allowing you to identify potential problems. Data quality processes are often needed but not yet in place. Although out of scope for the data scientist, you can advise on the need and added value of such processes.

2. **Business needs before tech needs**

   Many data scientists have a mathematics, statistics, or programming background and often have an operational mindset. Something that regularly goes wrong in business cases is that technical people start doing what is technically the best and start sidetracking the lines defined by business projects. Although this is very understandable, it is important to always keep in mind why companies are investing in a specific technology, which is, 99% of the time, to make a return on investing. When working in tech, it is important to keep in mind whether your technical topics are helping the company to reach its objectives, as you may lose funding quickly in the opposite case.

3. **Business metrics are key to a project succeeding**

   Helping a company reach its goals is often not even enough. You must also be able to prove to your company's leaders that you are indeed making them money or reaching their goals. To prove this, metrics are your best friend. As long as you define your project's key performance indicators from the outset and throughout, you can assure continuing support for your project, allowing you to work on cutting-edge technology.

4. **Be compatible and make company guidelines your own guidelines**

   Long-term successful projects will at some point be evaluated in terms of your company's best practices. If you want to ensure you have long-term relevance to your company, you need to make sure to keep in mind what your company is doing on a general level and make sure that what you do is compatible with this. Allowing incompatibility with the overall architecture is to set yourself up for failure.

5. **Technical metrics are great for avoiding problems**

   When projects become large, it may become difficult to maintain a full overview of everything that is running in your production environment. In the same way, as business metrics are used, you can set up technical metrics that help you keep a quick and easy overview of all the things you have and how they are doing. The larger your projects become, the more important monitoring will be, but the harder it will be to implement. The best practice is therefore to implement monitoring as soon as possible.

6. **Don't reinvent the wheel**

   Many data scientists and machine learning engineers are technology enthusiasts with our own ideas and vision on how to implement certain functionalities. One thing to keep in mind, though, is to avoid reinventing the wheel. When solutions already exist, be it in the company or outside, it is often useful to investigate whether it is possible to reuse them instead of "re-inventing the wheel" by developing the exact same functionality again.

The next section will guide you in furthering your knowledge and skills in the field of streaming analytics.

Going further

The focus of this book has been on giving you the tools necessary to get a quick introduction to the field of streaming analytics and has relatively quickly moved on to online machine learning algorithms for data science.

If you want to go further in streaming analytics, there are generally two directions in which you could start your journey: depth-first or breadth-first.

The depth-first approach consists of going even more in depth into online machine learning than the current book has been able to do. Although you should now have a solid basis in online machine learning, there is always more to learn. A number of useful resources for this follow:

- Keeping up with the general field of machine learning on the scientific side:

  - `https://paperswithcode.com/`
  - `https://arxiv.org/list/stat.ML/recent`

- Keeping up with a lot of practitioners that love sharing what they do:

  - `https://towardsdatascience.com/`

  - `https://neptune.ai/blog`

  - `https://www.kdnuggets.com/`

- Follow influential data scientists and machine learning practitioners on social networks such as the following:

  - LinkedIn

  - Twitter

- Practice your skills with tools such as the following:

  - Kaggle and other machine learning competitions

  - Hackathons

The breadth-first approach would suggest that you focus on auxiliary domains first, to have an all-around mastery of the architecture topics, data engineering, code efficiency, and the like. The following resources may be helpful for a journey in this direction:

- Look into cloud architecture and obtain certifications for the most popular ones:

  - `https://aws.amazon.com/certification/`

  - `https://cloud.google.com/certification`

- Improve your coding skills:

  - Codewars, HackerRank, and other competitive coding tools

  - Open source contributions

- Learn new tools and environments:

  - Learn machine learning in PySpark.

  - Learn machine learning in R.

  - Learn machine learning in Julia.

  - Databricks.

  - Dataiku.

  - AWS SageMaker.

The focus is quite different between the two directions. At the end of your journey, you may want to consider your insight into both directions. The direction that is most relevant for you will always depend on your personal objectives.

Summary

In this final chapter, you have seen a list of best practices that will help you to be successful and efficient while implementing this theory in practice. Finally, you have seen two potential learning paths that you may want to follow when continuing your learning journey into streaming analytics and online models.

With this, we have come to the end of this book. I hope that the book has been useful to you and that you will be successful in applying the topics in practice. It was a pleasure writing about this topic, which I am sure is going to gain a lot of traction soon. It will be one of the topics to look out for in the next trends of data science and machine learning. Of course, feel free to follow the publisher and me online for many new materials on streaming, data science, and more related topics to be published soon.

Index

Packt>

Other Books You May Enjoy

If you enjoyed this book, you may be interested in these other books by Packt:

Azure Databricks Cookbook

Phani Raj, Vinod Jaiswal

ISBN: 9781789809718

- Read and write data from and to various Azure resources and file formats
- Build a modern data warehouse with Delta Tables and Azure Synapse Analytics
- Explore jobs, stages, and tasks and see how Spark lazy evaluation works
- Handle concurrent transactions and learn performance optimization in Delta tables

- Learn Databricks SQL and create real-time dashboards in Databricks SQL

- Integrate Azure DevOps for version control, deploying, and productionizing solutions with CI/CD pipelines

- Discover how to use RBAC and ACLs to restrict data access

- Build end-to-end data processing pipeline for near real-time data analytics

The Artificial Intelligence Infrastructure Workshop

Bas Geerdink, Anand N.S., Kunal Gera, Gareth Dwyer

ISBN: 9781800209848

- Get to grips with the fundamentals of artificial intelligence

- Understand the importance of data storage and architecture in AI applications

- Build data storage and workflow management systems with open source tools

- Containerize your AI applications with tools such as Docker

- Discover commonly used data storage solutions and best practices for AI on Amazon Web Services (AWS)

- Use the AWS CLI and AWS SDK to perform common data tasks

Packt is searching for authors like you

If you're interested in becoming an author for Packt, please visit `authors.packtpub.com` and apply today. We have worked with thousands of developers and tech professionals, just like you, to help them share their insight with the global tech community. You can make a general application, apply for a specific hot topic that we are recruiting an author for, or submit your own idea.

Share Your Thoughts

Now you've finished *Machine Learning for Streaming Data with Python*, we'd love to hear your thoughts! Scan the QR code below to go straight to the Amazon review page for this book and share your feedback or leave a review on the site that you purchased it from.

`https://packt.link/r/1-803-24836-X`

Your review is important to us and the tech community and will help us make sure we're delivering excellent quality content.

Made in the USA
Columbia, SC
26 June 2023

19411086R00141